# DIRTY LITTLE SECRETS OF FAMILY BUSINESS

D0167884

## HENRY HUTCHESON

ISBN: 1941870007
ISBN 13: 9781941870006
Library of Congress Control Number: 2014911150
CreateSpace Independent Publishing Platform,
North Charleston, South Carolina

INDIE BOOKS INTERNATIONAL, LLC
2424 VISTA WAY, SUITE 316
OCEANSIDE, CA 92054
www.indiebooksintl.com

# CONTENTS

# ACKNOWLEDGEMENTS

This book is a compilation of many years of work, tremendous research, and extensive engagements helping family businesses find the answers that are best for them. While academicians, business leaders, and professionals can all gain insights from *Dirty Little Secrets*, its true audience is those currently running family businesses, and those in the next generation who may one day be running the family business. Thus, while each chapter attempts to address the various broad questions facing all family businesses, the perspective does alter between these two points of view.

Clearly none of this would have been possible without a lot of help. I would like to thank the Family Firm Institute (FFI) organization and members, my Institute of Management Consultants (IMC) group, the Society of Financial Services Professionals, the Wake Forest family business program, the editors of all the McClatchy papers, IGC and its members, the Psychodynamics of Family Business group, and the Kure Beach Professional Society.

On a personal level, let me thank my brother Jim who brought me into the family business profession and showed me the ropes; Jane Hilburt-Davis my FFI mentor; and Dane Huffman who helped me break into the professional writing field. Let me, of course, thank my family, Oskar, Avery, and Kirsten, for their patience with my travel schedule, and Kirsten in particular for her many hours of editing. Finally, I must thank those without whom this book truly would not have been possible, those family businesses that I have spent so much time with, especially Eddie, Mark, Kevin, Kayle, Mercer, Lisa, Kermit, and Lily.

# PREFACE

I recently attended my twentieth reunion at Columbia Business School. For two days we attended lectures from a variety of prominent professors and distinguished alumni.

While there were a variety of sessions, there was a definite theme coming from the weekend: Where will the jobs come from in the future? Professor Bruce Greenwald, touted as one of the top finance professors in the country, began his lecture by saying, "You all had better get used to your kids living at home with you for a long time to come." He then went on to describe the enormous imbalance in savings rates between those with the top 20 percent of income versus the bottom 80 percent. That bottom 80 percent is actually at a negative savings rate.

Diving even deeper, Andrew L. Stern, Senior Fellow at the Columbia Richard Paul Richman Center, and Presidential appointee to the Simpson-Bowles commission stated it more bluntly: "If anyone has an idea where our kids and grandkids are going to work in the future, please let me know." Through the course of his lecture he displayed a terrifying graph. Essentially, it showed that since 1940, Gross Domestic Product (GDP) and productivity have increased every year up until today. Wages have also increased, but for the first time started diverging around 2004. Employment has also remained steady through all these years, but then began diverging in 2008.

We think this is the subprime mortgage debacle. While it compounded the problem, the real issue is technology. We are replacing jobs with technology at such a rate that there simply will not be enough jobs to go around in the future on a global basis. That's right—*global* basis. In Europe there are fast food restaurants where you are greeted by an ATM to order your food; how long before they are in Bangladesh? 3D printers are making all sorts of machine parts; how long until everything is simply printed?

Dirty little secret #1: Having a family business is a wonderful advantage. You control your destiny, you can invest for the long-term, and it can be a tremendous resource for the next generation, whether it provides work experience for them to get jobs elsewhere, work within the family business, or is simply a financial resource to care for the well-being of your family. If you have a family business, it is important to work hard—and smart—to ensure its success from one generation to the next.

# SECTION I

*The Mystery that is Family Business*

Stop it right now, or I'll turn this car around!

# CHAPTER 1

## The Relative Problems of Family Business

"Happy families are all alike; every unhappy family is unhappy in its own way." So begins Leo Tolstoy's classic novel, *Anna Karenina*.

The same is true for the unhappy family business; every unhappy family business is unhappy in its own way. The root causes of the unhappiness, and the solutions, are the dirty little secrets of family business.

And yet, family businesses form the backbone of the economy in the United States and virtually every country of the world. The Family Firm Institute estimates that more than 70 percent of all businesses are family businesses. At the same time, family businesses historically have accounted for the largest portion of new jobs created, a significant percentage of the Gross Domestic Product (GDP), and a good chunk of Fortune 500 companies.

What is a family business exactly? Some define it as simply two or more relatives working in the same company. Another school of thought attributes family business status when there is significant family influence. Many think that "family business" simply means "small business." But the billion-dollar companies of Ford, Walmart, and Cargill would disagree. The best definition I have encountered comes from Carmen Bianchi, the director of the Family Business

Center at San Diego State University, who says, "A family business is any business that considers itself to be a family business."

There are also definitions of the generations of a family business. The first is referred to as the "founding generation," the second as a "sibling partnership," and the third as a "cousins' consortium." I usually refer to the fourth generation as "Wow, isn't that amazing," as only a small percentage of diligent and forward-thinking family businesses ever make it that far.

Family businesses, like relatives, come in many shapes and sizes. Most family businesses begin with a single founder, who either saw an opportunity or simply took action to make ends meet. Maybe it was both. However, this can quickly turn into a husband and wife team, or two brothers or sisters. Many family businesses are owned and run by women, who have the additional burden and conflict of being mom and the chief emotional support for the family.

Then the next generation comes along, grows up among the hustle and bustle of their parents trying to build a business, helps out where possible, and one day finds that they are working in their parents' business. Then the kids get married and bring in-laws into the business. Trusted and capable nonfamily employees are picked up along the way.

Regardless of the definition or form, there can be no greater joy than working with the people you love the most. Why are family businesses so challenging? Family is about unconditional love, and business is about profit. Dirty little secret: These two goals do not always align.

### Why do family businesses matter?

You would think that it is because there are a lot of them, and you would be correct. As I mentioned, over 70 percent of all businesses are family businesses, and they account for a significant number of new jobs and a large portion of GDP. However, what is perhaps more important is that so many are being created every day. Most businesses are begun by an individual who will then drag in other family members, or whose family members will jump in, seeing an opportunity. With more than 500,000 new businesses starting each year in the United States, the genesis of more than 1,000 family businesses are created every day.

Warren Buffett, arguably the world's greatest investor, touched on his passion for family businesses in his 2009 letter to shareholders: "Our long avowed goal is to be the buyer of choice for businesses - particularly those built and owned by families. ...We have a decided advantage, therefore, when we encounter sellers who truly care about their businesses." If Warren Buffett thinks they matter, who are we to argue?

### What makes them special?

We must also understand that they are different and unique from nonfamily businesses in that there is a permanent emotional relationship with your work colleague. Families are lifelong social structures, characterized by unqualified love and support among its members. You can quit your job, but you can't quit your family.

Which brings us to another great statistic of family businesses: Many studies have shown that family businesses can actually outperform nonfamily businesses. The reasons for this phenomenon are plentiful. Yes, people try harder when the family name is on the sign. Yes, family businesses have a longer-term perspective than the quarterly driven publicly held nonfamily businesses. And yes, you can use your kids as slave labor and get away with it!

But the top factor that enables family businesses to rise to the top must be the level of trust. Each member of the family knows every other member is doing their best to move the company forward. As Professor John Whitney of Columbia Business School stated in his book, *The Trust Factor*, "Imagine the performance of your company if everyone knew what, when, and how to do everything, did it correctly and on time, all in alignment with the company mission."

But what happens when trust breaks down? Or when one of the family members is either not willing or able to perform at the requisite level? There can be a sense of entitlement, there can be drug abuse, and there can be simple laziness. This forces the other family members to either pretend to ignore the problem or ask the profoundly awkward question, "How do I fire my son/daughter/brother?" The former is bad for business, the latter bad for the family.

This is the reason professionalizing the family business early is so important. It helps move the business in the right direction while removing the inherent personal nature of a family business. However, it can be difficult.

A business starts when the founder strikes upon an idea or opportunity for a business. To survive and grow, decisions must be made quickly, chances must be taken, and mistakes will occur. Hence, once a level of success and stability is achieved, there is no manual on how to run the business; it is "all up here in my head."

Nonetheless, for a family business to be successful long-term, it *must put forth effort* in some key areas: communication, governance, management succession and planning.

Fortunately there is help: publications like *Family Business Magazine* and *Family Business Journal*. University-based family business centers around the country do research that family businesses can join. There is also the Family Firm Institute, the global governing body of professionals who serve family businesses. The institute is dedicated to being a resource for family businesses and providing education and certification to those who serve family businesses.

And then there are, of course, family business consultants who assist these businesses with their issues, like my firm, Family Business USA. Our firm was founded on the idea that family businesses can benefit from getting professional help. How did I first learn of the dirty little secrets of family business? I grew up working for my family's business, Olan Mills Portrait Studios, the predominant provider of family photography around the United States. The company was founded by my grandfather, Olan Mills. My two uncles took it over for the next generation. While my brother seemed very happy working in our family business, I decided to make my own path by pursuing a global management career with IBM.

## Apex Family Shares the Secrets of Their Business Success

Have you ever seen those guys hanging from the sides of buildings while cleaning windows 50 floors up and think they are crazy? You wouldn't think that of Apex-based family business Scotties Building Services, which is one of the 10 largest window-cleaning companies in the country.

Scotties is truly a rags-to-riches story. Back in 1986, John McGrath, who grew up working in the window-cleaning business with his dad in Syracuse, New York, decided to get out of the snow and move south to North Carolina. Once he was settled, he sent for his dad to come down, and soon after his brother Tom left the military and came down, and they formed a new window-cleaning business.

The window-cleaning business was different back then. "It was like the Wild West. Some crazy guys with a bucket of soap and a wiper could get jobs hanging off buildings cleaning," John McGrath said. "It's not like that anymore."

John and Tom McGrath were founding members of the International Window Cleaning Association, whose charter is to promote safety and education, and enhance professionalism throughout the industry. Scotties went about cleaning up the cleaning industry. And the family led by example by professionalizing themselves. A lot of this came about by reading a book, *The E Myth*, by Michael Gerber.

### Work on Your Business

"The point of *The E Myth* is to spend time working on your business, not just in your business," Tom McGrath said. "It teaches you how to put systems and controls in place, and that's what we did at Scotties." And it paid off. The cleaning industry has very low barriers to entry, and there are no legal certifications required to operate. The key to success is to be safe, efficient, economical and consistent. In fact, this is the company's motto. Developing a reputation is the key to success. With a 96 percent retention rate, it looks like it is paying off.

The dedication to safety extended so far that they formed another company focusing exclusively on designing and manufacturing safety harnesses for high-rise building cleaners.

The McGrath family also has spent time working on being a family business. They have divided the functional areas among the three of them with John in charge of sales and marketing, Tom focusing on management and operations, and dad providing the initial expertise required to do the actual work. It is a known family business management tenet that the clearer the definition of roles and responsibilities, the better.

### Trust Each Other

But what happens when disagreements occur? "We talk it out, but ultimately the decision falls to the one who has responsibility for that particular area, and we just trust each other," Tom McGrath said. What also helps is a strong staff. They have four geographic divisions with a general manager running each with a great deal of autonomy. "Having a strong management team provides another good source of input for decision making," Tom McGrath said.

Another trick they learned to help them work well together as a family business is that they try to keep business talk to business hours. And they consciously avoid taking on issues toward the end of the work day. "Any issues that come up late in the day, we just save them for tomorrow," John McGrath said.

Today, in addition to their key managers, Scotties has the third brother, Gary, in the business, as well as John's son and Tom's son-in-law. Tom and John both pointed out that most of the successful companies in their industry were family businesses.

So remember, the next time you see some guys hanging from the side of a skyscraper, they are not crazy, they are just Scotties!

### Five Rules for Family Business Success

Research shows that two out of three family businesses do not survive into the next generation. And not just from the first generation to the second, but from any generation to the next.

There is a lot of information available on what the central causes are for family business failures – and thus, some guidelines on how to avoid them. In this book we will address the top success strategies for those family businesses that do survive and even thrive. Briefly, here are the key rules:

1.  *Keep the lines of communication open.* Communication is critical. When I once asked publisher Steve Forbes at a CEO Forum what advice he would give to family businesses, he declared that communication was the most important element to success for his family's business. McKay Belk, grandson of the founder of Belk retail stores, and Frank Holding Jr., the CEO of the family-controlled First Citizens Bank, both agreed. It is also important to be proactive: Schedule family meetings to discuss topics such as business transition, business performance, and responsibilities. Most of all, don't let issues fester.

2.  *Assign clear roles and responsibilities.* As a family member, there is a natural tendency to feel everything is my business. However, not everything is every family member's responsibility. Without job definitions, family members will be on top of each other working the same problem. Elaine Voci, founder of the family business Voci Spa, agrees: "It is important that each family member have clearly defined roles in order to operate smoothly."

3.  *Keep good financial data.* The downfall of many small businesses and family businesses is not having solid data. "Accurate financial data is essential, especially when you are trying to raise capital in a fast-growing industry like we are," said Sally Crowell of Crowell Systems, which provides software to health care clients. I had a client who

predicted a 3-4 percent net income increase at year end, only to learn that the company was down 2 percent because of incompetent accounting. All the plans that were being made for growth had to be redirected to cost savings. Good financial data is like a clean windshield: it lets you know exactly where you are.

4. *Avoid overpaying family members.* Market-based compensation is fundamental and essential. Parents in family businesses tend to overpay the next generation, or pay them the same. Both are bad practices. A family business I worked with paid each of the four family members the same salary, even though they had very different responsibilities. Certainly the president should receive higher compensation than his brother who, while quite good, was a blueprint designer. The longer unfair compensation practices continue, the messier it will be to clean up when it blows up.

5. *Don't hire relatives if they are unqualified.* Competence is key. Family businesses are a conundrum: The family aspect generates unqualified love, while the business side cares about profits. Thus, family members will be hired to give them a job, even though they are not qualified. The remedy is to get them trained, move them to a role that matches their skills, or have them leave.

High-functioning family businesses can outperform nonfamily businesses on a number of metrics. Trust is the driver. But when trust breaks down, the business suffers, placing a significant strain on family harmony. Adhering to the above five rules, while uncomfortable, can keep a family and business on the track to success and help avoid being one of those that does not survive.

### *What to Do When Your Child Says, "I Want In on the Business"*

If you are reading this book, then you probably have the pleasure of working with your family every day. (Yes, I said pleasure.) And certainly one of the greatest joys for parents is the opportunity to have their children working in their business. However, just as good parents know letting their children pursue their immediate wants and desires won't result in growing into confident and responsible adults, parents cannot let junior loose in the family business and expect him to end up with the business savvy and people skills to take the company to the next level.

The foundation of any successful family business involving the children is an understanding that the children aren't being forced into the business. Not only can pushing them into the business create resentment, leading to animosity, it can create apathy and lackluster performance.

I had a client who told his son that if he didn't join the business, they would sell it. Not wanting to deal with the guilt, he decided to join the company. Now, the fact that he was forced to join the business is brought out during every contentious conversation.

If you're running a great business, where the financial rewards, work environment, and free time all look good to you, it can be difficult to understand why your children aren't excited about jumping on board. However, in the end, forcing your children to join the business won't move it forward, and you may be depriving them of pursuing their true passions.

That said, if your children want to be involved in your business, how do you make sure it's the right fit?

I had the opportunity to meet Julie Logan, Owner of Logan's Trading Company, one of the country's top family owned garden centers. In our conversation, she mentioned that her daughter Leslie had joined the business some time ago, so I asked her how it was working out. She said it was going well, as Leslie seemed to have "a knack and a passion" for the business. Indeed, these are the two base requirements for future success and leadership in any business.

What is also inherent in this discussion is that the children need to learn the business. Certainly, anyone who works at a company for a number of years is going to expand her level of understanding and ability to manage certain parts of the business as necessary. But a family business is a little different since there is the thought that your children may take over one day. They should be proactively prepared for this possibility.

The first thing to consider is education. This doesn't mean they need a doctorate degree, but they should have an education appropriate to the industry or field. The next recommendation for equipping your children to be effective in the business may seem counterproductive: They need to spend some time working outside your company. Not only will they gain some work experience, but the experience they get will be different from your business. However, these are actually secondary benefits. The real impact lies in working for another company where they don't have a priority communication line to the owners, and their family name is not on the building. That's right, they're just like everyone else, and they will be judged solely on their performance. The result of this is a major psychological shift, where they become their own people and grow to understand they're solely in control of their own lives and are responsible for the outcome. It's not critical that they work in the exact same industry, but it certainly would be good.

Another proactive step in the process is mentoring. Don't confuse mentoring with simply teaching. Mentoring is the informal process of working one on one with someone to help them become adept in all aspects of a particular field. But before you begin, lay the groundwork. You need to sit down with your children and make a declaration that you would like to enter a mentoring process with them to try to pass on the skills and knowledge you have about running the business. It also needs to be understood that you're not the perfect mentor, so everything won't be perfect. Also, point out that the mentoring is from your point of view. Once what you share is mastered, they will be expected to build upon this base. At the same time, the mentee must also be open and willing to be mentored, and commit to being patient with the mentor through the process.

Having a qualified key employee as a mentor is also effective. The personal connection is not there, which may lead to easier and more honest communication. Moreover, this can be good preparation for the future relationship between the key employee and his potential future boss.

The final piece of sage advice on dealing with your children in the business is to give them a little leeway to pursue their own ideas. Many times, parents in family businesses dismiss ideas coming from their children because they think their children lack the maturity, experience or knowledge to know what they are talking about. Many times, this is true. However, there are times when your children's ideas have potential merit. Giving them the leeway to pursue some of their ideas, as uncomfortable as it may be, will help them grow and build greater trust with you - and just may result in increased business.

### It's Time to Open the Door to the Next Generation's Ideas

When most family-owned companies are started, no one is thinking about how the business will continue into the next generation. The focus is on getting the business off the ground and stabilized to generate a reliable return. With one estimate showing that 50 percent of new businesses will fail in five years, and more than 70 percent in ten years, the odds are intimidating. The risk for founders is high.

However, through the years, the creative, persistent and sometimes risky problem solving that is the secret to success is often abandoned as the business grows. The more success that is gained, the less risk the owner is willing to take on. This can lead to stagnation, rigidity and even decline, unless steps are taken and the owner remains flexible.

For a company to be successful into the next generation, new ideas are essential. The world around us is always changing, and it takes a level of creativity to keep up. For example, one family-owned retailer I know swears that establishing a dog food business inside their garden supply store has been instrumental in maintaining long-term relevance. And we all know of retailers that have incorporated food services in order to bring in more customers. While these two ideas may not be right for your store, you need to create an environment in which other new ideas are welcome.

The obstacle to creating this kind of open-mindedness lies both with the owner and the next generation.

The difficulty with the owner is that, as time goes on, there is a psychological and rational reason to begin consolidating and securing for the future. Ever increasingly, growth stocks are moved into bonds or dividend-bearing equities. Owners are inherently reluctant to change the business, and are resistant to radical change. But ideas about change lead to actual change only if they are not stomped out.

Let's look at family business owners. They are in charge. As the leaders, they can best see how a change here could impact something over there. They have years of experience and have seen what does and doesn't work. They built the business - it's their baby, and they're depending on the income.

For the next generation, bringing an idea to the table can be quite intimidating. It probably will not be perfect, and all of the cons will be pointed out. Feelings can easily get hurt, and discouragement can set in.

At one company I worked with, I began to notice one of the senior managers seemed disinterested in discussions about the future. When I asked why, the response was, "I tried to get involved when I first started, but I got my hand slapped so many times, I decided to just focus on my work. And since I'm retiring in the next ten years, whatever happens can't really affect me."

If the owner is truly interested in the company moving forward, it is necessary to begin handing over some control and allow the next generation to get the creative juices flowing and shape it in their own way. But the problem with the next generation is that years of doing things the owner's way may inhibit ingenuity.

To foster an atmosphere of openness and originality, it is important for the owner to understand where the next generation is coming from, including these considerations:

- The next generation is going to have their own style, which will be different from yours. But that doesn't make it bad. In fact, research shows it's good. The future is different from the past, and the style of the past may not be effective in the future.

- The next generation needs to make it their own. The difference between the passenger seat and the driver's seat has a profound psychological impact.

- The next generation needs to develop their strengths. This can only happen if they are given some free reign to make mistakes.

Still, after years of being the head honcho, it can be difficult to begin to let go. Here are some steps an owner can take to stand back and build up the next generation:

- Allow the next generation to run with some ideas. This must be done in an intelligent manner, of course. Start small, provide input, but let them run with it while making yourself available for help.

- Encourage them. As a regular course of business, major corporations like IBM conduct brainstorming sessions. Give employees advance notice that there will be such a session. Set the date, announce the rules and commence.

- The rules are: Don't allow criticism, encourage wild ideas, go for quantity, and combine and/or improve on others' ideas. The golden rule is that the owner must remain quiet. If you want to make it even better, have the next generation run the session. You can tee it up so that everyone knows you support it, but then leave the room.

Convey everything I have written above to the next generation, and declare this to be your goal. The next generation has been toiling under your tutelage for many years. At the beginning, it was pure command and control. Over time, some responsibilities were handed over, and they may now be running certain parts of the company--heck, they may be running all of it. But they may be doing nothing more than cranking the crank the exact same way the first generation did for thirty years. The years of pounding into their brain "how it is done" has inherently suppressed parts of the brain that contemplate "how it *could* be done."

Ask the next generation to develop the strategic plan. In the field of family business and next generation prep work, there are multiple requirements that must be met to some degree for the next generation to be successful. The next to the last one is strategic development. What is the strategy over the next five, ten, twenty years? Placing this bombshell on the lap of the next generation can help to break them out of "follower" mode and move them into "leadership" mode.

Ask how they are going to significantly increase the revenue of the business. This is closely aligned to the strategic plan, but has a sharper point on it. While the strategic plan meshes the company with the world around it, figuring out how to impact the revenue instills practicality in the process.

Implement ideas through pilots. Once you've opened Pandora's Box, you may not be able to shut it again. No problem. If there is an idea out there, do a pilot--a small-scale version of the idea where you can validate whether the idea has real merit or not while minimizing risk and cost.

Innovation has been and always will be the game changer. It must be balanced with efficient operations. But the long-term success of your family business is predicated on creating an environment where the next generation has their antennas up and minds working on new ideas to improve and grow the business.

### Logan Trading Company Just Keeps on Growing

Logan Trading Company is a highly successful garden center in the United States. It is also a third-generation family business that has seen its share of ups and downs, but has managed to stay on course and thrive.

In 1965 Robert M. "Bob" Logan founded the company, primarily as a produce buyer. He quickly expanded his business to include garden products and brokering damaged railroad goods. Located in Raleigh, North Carolina at the old Farmers Market off Capital Boulevard, his business grew, and he found that his success was centering on garden products.

### Family and business

Along the way, Bob and his wife, Helen, raised a large family: five girls and one boy named Robert M. Logan Jr. Like many family businesses, all his kids spent time working in the business. However, Robert Logan remembers that his dad was always pressuring him to join the business full time. Robert thought he should be allowed to make up his own mind and pursue his own dream: joining the ministry. He enrolled in Southeastern Seminary.

While attending school he worked outside the business with his cousin doing landscaping. And it was during this time he was not working for his father and pursuing his own path, he had an epiphany: There are other ways to minister outside of being in the ministry, and he loved working with plants. In 1974, Robert decided to join his father full time.

### Crossing the chasm

In 1990, the state decided to expand the Farmers Market and moved it to another part of town. This did not sit well with Robert as it would take him too far from his current customer base. Scouring the area for a suitable location, he came across an abandoned railroad station near town.

The structure was in disrepair. Homeless people were living in it, and it was surrounded by abandoned buildings. There were weeds and overgrowth everywhere, it was near low-income housing and noisy trains came through all the time. So not only would it take substantial money and effort to bring the site up to par, what customer in her right mind would want to shop here? His family and friends thought he was crazy - except for one.

Greg Poole and Bob had done some business in the past, and Robert had the opportunity to get to know Greg at an early age. By an amazing coincidence, or simply by providence, Greg approached Robert independently with an idea that he should relocate Logan's to the old railroad station, and that he would help him do it.

So in 1991, with some hard work and a lot of advertising informing customers of the new location, Logan's opened its new store. Maybe two wrongs don't make a right, but just maybe two crazy people with vision make a genius.

### The family problem

Dirty little secret: One of the top reasons family businesses fail is having too many shareholders. It is worse if many are not working in the business and have the majority ownership. Robert found himself in that situation when his father died in 1984. In essence, Bob was not in full control of the business. In 2009, with family members getting older and Robert winning praise as the leader of the business, all the shares were consolidated underneath him.

He decided to close on Sundays, as it is a day of rest. Robert also decided to revive the old diner at the new location, and there has been a line for lunch ever since.

Bob and Julie have run Logan's over the years, and their two kids, Josh and Leslie, have grown up working in the business. However, based on Bob's philosophy of life, there is no pressure for them to be a part of the business. He would rather they pursue their own dreams.

Josh wants to help underprivileged children in Brazil, and Leslie has a passion for music. Some years ago Josh was the general manager for Logan's, with Leslie working for him. Now Leslie is acting as general manager with Josh underneath her. It is looking like the Logan family tradition will continue into the next generation, still being able to pursue their dreams, while providing a gardening oasis for their customers at the same time.

# SECTION II

*Family*

# CHAPTER 2

## Conflict Resolution Before Family Revolution

Working in a business is tough. Employees are trying to get ahead, develop their skills, and impress their boss. Most likely they are competing with a coworker for advancement. At the same time, managers and owners are trying to develop and execute successful strategies while trying to groom their employees. And this whole dance occurs in an environment of aggressive competitors, choosy customers, and margin-squeezed suppliers.

Now imagine that this business is a family business with a mom, dad, son, daughter, son-in-law, and maybe a nephew, all with different skills, life goals, and relationships with each other. No wonder more than 65 percent of all family businesses don't succeed to the next generation. Communication is the key to success for any family business. In this chapter we'll discuss some effective strategies for keeping communication open and dealing with difficult problems that may arise.

### *Effective Family Meetings*

In a seminar some years ago, I asked Steve Forbes, editor of *Forbes* magazine and family business icon, his advice for family businesses.

His answer was communication. "Our family has a mandatory meeting every three weeks where we all meet for coffee for ninety minutes for the purpose of bringing up any issues anyone might have," he said.

If it is working for Forbes, it would probably work for you too. Family meetings are a great way to improve communication in a family business. Some thought and planning are required to be effective, but they can be fun and are invaluable to the success of the business and the family. Here is a guide to how to run these meetings in the best way possible.

***When in doubt, include everyone:*** Clearly you include the family members in the business, regardless of their role. Yes, maybe the cousin is working on the factory floor, or maybe your sister is only part time. You may also need those who are not working in the business, but are directly related, and spouses. Exclusion can create animosity and suspicion, and partners are typically the closest confidants, and strongest influencers, to the working family members.

***Start with developing a Family Manual:*** The purpose of this manual is to lay the ground rules of how the meetings will take place to ensure that everyone gets a chance to be heard, and that behaviors that impede communication are left outside. The key is that it must be created from scratch by the family members themselves.

***Active listening:*** Many people think this phrase means to pay attention, but that is only part of the definition. The other part is to prove it. This is done by paraphrasing back to the speaker what you think you just heard and asking them if you understood correctly. This does not mean you necessarily agree with them. But without knowing they have been heard, the discussion grinds to a halt. The Harvard Program on Negotiations includes active listening as a core module.

*Hold meetings regularly:* They can be weekly, monthly, quarterly, etc. But the important thing is for everyone to know when the next meeting will occur. Left open-ended, family members with issues to discuss can feel that others want to avoid their topic, and animosity can build toward whoever is responsible for scheduling the meeting. Either have a regular schedule or schedule the next meeting at the end of every meeting.

*Plan the meeting:* Be sure to allocate enough time for the meeting, give everyone a chance to put their item on the agenda before the meeting, and leave time for open discussion. By doing this, everyone can be assured of getting a chance to speak and be heard.

*Facilitator:* Family meetings can become awkward if there is a disagreement. Other family members will jump in, or get dragged in, and try to resolve the impasse with good intentions. Unfortunately, this usually results in the feeling that "people are taking sides." Moreover, as the designated or default coordinator has some power, suspicion of their true motives can exist. An experienced facilitator who has no vested interest in the outcome can help keep family meetings on track.

*Incorporate some fun:* It doesn't have to be much, but something that reminds everyone that we are here because we want to be, not because we have to be. You could begin each meeting with each person recounting an interesting encounter since the last meeting. Or ask an amusing question to answer, such as, "What five foods would you want if stranded on an island?" Everyone can answer or you can simply rotate turns at each meeting.

### Resolving Conflicts without Destroying the Family or the Business

Dirty little secret: Although family meetings can be a great tool, they are not a cure-all. It is inevitable that problems will arise and you must be prepared to deal with them in a way that will preserve your relationships without harming the business.

### Conflicts with Your Children

What do you do when your son or daughter bristles at you asking him or her to perform some task –and the other employees notice? Parent-child conflicts are generally par for the course in any family business, as you are mixing a "family system" with a "business system."

A family system is geared toward one thing: unconditional love and support. We've all seen the mother on the news being interviewed about her son who's been convicted of some crime, saying, "He really is a good boy." What is also important to note is that a family is a system, which means all of the parts are interconnected. Just considering a mom, dad, son and daughter, there are 12 one-way connections. And as in any system, a change in one area can have an impact on a completely different area. At the same time, parents are working together to train their children to become responsible and self-sufficient adults, and ultimately set a foundation of habits and beliefs that will result in their long-term happiness. And then there's the fact that parents simply want to enjoy their children. Families are more complicated than they may appear.

A business system, while equally complex, is virtually the opposite of a family system. The business exists to achieve a specific purpose, usually to increase shareholder value. Typically, the emotions and well-being of the employees come into consideration only to the extent that it improves or doesn't negatively impact the overall objective. This doesn't mean you can't have a wonderful—and profitable—work environment where everyone is happy. But we all know that everyone would be *unhappy* if your business went under and they lost their jobs.

What happens when you mix these two systems together? It depends on the degree that you allow the family system to enter the business system. While you can't deny or ignore the fact that you work with your family, if you're in business, you must put the business first, and keep family issues out of your company.

Why is your son or daughter having an issue with carrying out the task? It could be for a variety of reasons, and thus the answers to deal with the situation can vary.

**The child is having an issue at home:** Perhaps he wrecked the family car or got into an argument with you about something non-business-related. Whatever the issue, he brought it to work. When you ask him to perform a reasonable task, he bristles because he's harboring resentment for something going on in the family.
**Solution:** Take your son aside and tell him that he needs to adhere to the expectations of the company at work. If he has an issue at home, it should be left out of work and discussed at home.

**The parent is having an issue at home:** Maybe you are arguing with your spouse, and your daughter has gotten involved in the situation. When you come to work, you're the boss and are in a position to make unreasonable requests to your daughter in a show of retaliation.
**Solution:** Your daughter should take you aside and have the discussion about leaving family issues at home.

**The parent truly has an unreasonable request**: Maybe you like to give your son the dirty work to make him prove himself. Perhaps when there's a loose issue, you always turn to your son to clean it up rather than give it to the appropriate employee.

**Solution:** In this instance, your son needs to show some restraint in his reaction, and have a discussion with you about the issue. (Maybe the bristling has something to do with a particular nonfamily employee, and your son's reaction is to communicate to that employee that he's above the work and above his parent. This points to an issue of entitlement.)

**Entitlement:** If your son bristles when there are no issues at home, and the work being requested is a completely normal, then perhaps there's simply an issue of entitlement.

**Solution for issues related to entitlement:** The answer is more complex. This issue is never an isolated case, but rather something that has built over time. Likewise, the solution is something that must also be addressed over time. You must explain in no uncertain terms that you are the boss and they are the employees. And when a boss tells them to do something, they should either calmly and rationally propose a better course of action or perform the task.

### Entitlement: The Family Business Killer

When I read the headline, "P. Diddy Buys $360,000 Car for Son's 16th Birthday," I could not help but think: "What a way to mess up a kid, but I guess it's none of my business."

But if this type of thing had been applied in the world of family businesses, I would have thought, "There goes that business." After all, a sense of entitlement in a child may be the number one killer of a family business.

I would define entitlement as an attitude or behavior that you are deserving of respect and privilege beyond your skills, knowledge, and experience. We all know these kinds of people. But really, who cares? You can just avoid them or put up with them and get some of the fringe benefits of associating with these people. Wouldn't we all like to drive P. Diddy's son's car?

But believing you have the skills to run a business, when you don't, or thinking you can run the business because your dad did, are terrific ways to drive your family business into a brick wall. The marketplace does not care what your name is or how much money you have. The marketplace wants the best product and service for the best price. And if you can do this profitably, then you win. If you don't, you lose.

Entitled family business members can fail to listen to those who *do* have the necessary skills and experience. One business owner's son with a company in the western United States decided to bring all production in-house, over the vehement protests of the seasoned production manager and the CFO. This resulted in higher quality, but there was not enough work to justify the people or the equipment. The son thought that because his father was such a natural at business, so was he. He was wrong. Today they are out of business.

Raising a child with the appropriate balance of confidence and humility is certainly a challenge. Next time you are faced with a decision on this, just ask yourself, "What would P. Diddy do?" And then do the opposite.

Dirty little secret: While entitlement can come from many different places, the cause, and the place where change must begin, is typically with the parents.

Maybe the child was rarely told "no," or the parents have over-promised their child's future in the company and the rewards that await him. If the child has been allowed to assume he has special privileges and is above certain tasks, then the people to look at are the parents.

Dirty little secret: We are all familiar with the study that showed that the highest correlation to long life is to virtually starve yourself. The reason is that the body finds a way to function extremely efficiently with few resources. It is believed that the cure to entitlement is closely correlated: the founding generation started the business typically because they were broke and trying to make ends meet. They go into debt, live on a shoestring budget, until one day they actually make some money. Unfortunately, once the money comes, it gets showered on the next generation, so that their children don't have to suffer like they did. Perhaps it is this "suffering," however, that creates the required drive and focus to be successful.

Entitlement can also come from immaturity. If the child doesn't know what the real world is like and has had a fairly comfortable upbringing, he may simply have a misperception of the world. One of the great solutions to this is for the child to go out into the world—a job outside the family business.

In the short term, there's an easy answer that could be effective— firing your child. When I asked Greg Rohde, President of Green Sense, who has had two of his kids working for him at various times, what he did when this situation arose, he simply said, "I fired them. In fact, I have fired both of them multiple times now."

## *Conflicts with Your Parents*

One of the most difficult situations for you to handle as the next generation to take over the company is dealing with disagreements about the business with the current generation ownership. You're having an issue with someone who has been in the business longer than you have. They've seen and done more in the industry than you have. Therefore, when they have an opinion about something, they can, and many times do, resort to the simple phrase, "Yeah, we tried that before, and it didn't work."

I had a client whose son was relatively new to the business. However, he was bright, motivated and rational, and had outside work experience with a more sophisticated company. But as he made his way through the business, he would periodically have run-ins with his father, and it was driving him crazy. The issue was that although his father was out of the loop, he thought he could still sweep in at any moment and apply the business philosophy he previously created and followed.

The more common scenario is when the current generation is actually at the top of their game, but is still resistant to the next generation's ideas. When I went to work for IBM, I was in my mid-twenties, and, in reality, would consider myself a snot-nose kid. Nonetheless, the professionals I was supporting were insistent, "We want to hear your ideas because it will help us take a fresh look at what we are doing." Indeed, I did a lot of bumping around, trying to adjust from the theoretical world of academia to the practical realm of live global business. However, given license to ask stupid questions about why we did things a certain way added value to many of the business policies and procedures at the time.

Many times, the current generation cannot see the application of "boiled frogs." If you put a frog in boiling water, it will jump out. But, if you put it in room temperature water and slowly heat it up, the frog dies. The pace of change is so slow that they don't notice until it's too late—even if their son or daughter is yelling at them that the water is hot!

Because the current leadership has been around so long and has seen so much, these people can be prone to dismissing new or different ideas because they have already seen or considered them. And because they are busy, or the message is not articulated in a manner that will trigger all the right hot spots, they don't fully understand the message to actually consider it.

Dirty little secret: Another common route to heated discussions is when the current generation is intolerant of mistakes. Even worse is when they don't realize it. I had a client a while back who was irritated that his employees didn't take more initiative when it came to what appeared to be obvious things that needed to be done. They would always come to him for the final answer or approval on any action they wanted to pursue. When I asked him how willing he was to accept mistakes, he realized why no one was making a move without his approval.

So here you are, the bright-eyed and bushy-tailed next generation family member working in the business, wanting to find a way to add value and gain approval. You take an action you think will yield positive results, but, unfortunately, it doesn't turn out exactly right—and then you get chewed out. How do you think you are going to feel the next time you see an opportunity? You're not likely to pursue it in order to avoid the possible fallout if the results aren't perfect. It's also likely that you're going to have some suppressed anger about it.

Another odd, but common, factor is that mom or dad don't want to be shown up. It seems childish, but how will they feel if they have said, "No, no, no" to something for years, and then junior comes along and proves that it was a great idea. Everyone should be happy since progress is being made, but it's not always that way.

At the same time, remember, mom and dad may not be interested in leaving the business quite yet. Thus, there is the tricky process of moving them out of the leadership role and into a more functional role while continuing to have them advise on the business. If this is not recognized, there can be resistance to new ideas.

Up to this point, the discussion has revolved around understanding the actions and viewpoints of the current generation that could be counterproductive. But let's not forget that you, as the next generation to take over the business, have an equal, if not larger, role in the process. Ask yourself these questions:

1.  Are you experienced enough for your ideas to be valid?

2.  Are you approaching the current generation in a manner that is respectful of the legacy they've built?

3.  Are you working with the current generation and other key players to formulate a strong plan?

You've heard, "He who lives in a glass house should not throw stones." The point here is to be sure you have your own house in order before becoming too critical or adamant.

Here are some tips to deal constructively with the current generation when disagreements arise:

**Have a conversation.** Get an acknowledgement that you would like to add value to the business. Declare that you're not perfect, and not all your thoughts and actions will be perfect. Declare that you understand and respect the many years of experience of the current generation. Then, declare that with this understanding, you would like to be able to express your thoughts and ideas about various aspects of the business—and have them heard. Most importantly, both parties need to agree and acknowledge that sometimes you're going to disagree.

**Have an approach, and move at a pace that's appropriate to the weight of the issue.** If you want to make a minor price adjustment, discuss it over lunch. If you want to take an action involving tens or hundreds of thousands of dollars, then approach it in multiple stages over multiple meetings.

**Actively listen.** As mentioned previously, this means repeating back to the speaker what they said to the degree that they are convinced that you fully understand their point of view.

**Do not try to resolve issues once emotions have taken over.** Once adrenalin has dumped into the system, the rational brain virtually shuts down and animalistic defense mechanisms take over. If either one of you is in this state, only damage can occur. Stop and pick it up later.

**Communicate.** Many times, issues arise simply because neither party is fully aware of what the other person has been involved in. If too much time has gone by without a good one-on-one session about the business, you can run into trouble.

### Conflicts with Significant Others

I was surprised recently when, during a presentation to a local Rotary group, I was asked about a rather obscure family business dynamic. In seminars where I present case studies, I actually offer a prize to the person who can figure out this subtle family business dynamic. Although I did not include a case study in this talk, someone in the audience asked about it. This hidden dynamic is the influence of significant others.

In the family business context, a significant other is someone behind the main person, who is not present during discussions, who influences the actions and decisions of that person for his or her own purposes. The question I was asked was, "Do you ever find a situation where there are people who are not in the family business who are influencing decisions of those in the business?" The answer is not only yes, but actually, most of the time. And many times it extends beyond influence to virtual control.

I once worked with a family where the up-and-coming son appeared competent in the business, and said he wanted to run the business, but he did not convey a strong desire or passion about it. But whenever the subject turned to philosophy or art, he would light up like a Murano glass chandelier.

Sometime later in meeting with his mother, who did not work in the business, she declared that her son was the right person to take over the company. Interestingly, she attributed all the company's success to her husband's unique personality, and then described how her son's personality was, while admirable, virtually the opposite. It became clear that it was her dream for her son to take over the company. More important, she had been subtly pushing her son and husband to fulfill her dream.

These examples demonstrate the potential damage of significant others, where someone on the outside of the family business is driving his or her own agenda by influencing or manipulating someone working in the family business.

However, the positive side of this is when someone is providing advice and input to someone in the business to selflessly assist that person with their hopes, dreams, and goals within the family business. We all rely on the thoughts and counsel of family and friends when faced with big decisions and this is normal, healthy, and good.

It can, of course, become irritating, and potentially destructive, when family members inside the business receive too much input, all with the best of intentions. In this scenario, it might make sense to consider establishing a family council that can put some structure around all the opinions and advice.

What is important is to be able to understand and distinguish between friendly counsel intended to help you move forward, and the kind of advice that may be tainted with fulfilling someone else's dream, jealousy, or spite. What is always most important is to hold your own counsel and ultimately decide for yourself what is best for you.


## Conflicts Involving Dependency

There is one bad habit that is very difficult to break, and can find a warm home sometimes in family businesses: chemical dependency. Chemical dependency is certainly an uncomfortable topic to discuss, and one wonders how it fits into the realm of concern of family businesses – especially as it is not contained to just family businesses.

Dirty little secret: Indeed, it is estimated that up to 5 percent of the population in the United States may suffer from alcohol dependency and abuse. While it is probably the most popular "chemical" that is abused, there are, of course, many others.

Alcoholism is defined as, "A broad term for problems with alcohol, and is generally used to mean compulsive and uncontrolled consumption of alcoholic beverages, usually to the detriment of the drinker's health, personal relationships, and social standing. It is medically considered a disease." Of course what makes it difficult and awkward for many people is that it can be difficult to distinguish someone who is a heavy drinker from an alcoholic. We all remember that *Animal House*-type friend in college who would tie one on, get silly and be the life of the party, but then be one of the first ones up in the morning and ready to go. While at the time you may have been concerned about him, he is now happily married, with great kids, and a good job. (Unfortunately John Belushi was not that way, and died of a drug overdose.)

I know some people who enjoy drinking, but decide to abstain for the month of January to give their bodies a rest, and perhaps to check in with themselves to make sure something has not gotten a hold of them that they are not aware of.

No one knows exactly what causes alcoholism. Some think there is a possibility that it is inherited genetically; however, this has yet to be proven. Others think there is a correlation between drinking at an early age and alcoholism. Chris Kennedy Lawford, UN Goodwill Ambassador on Drug Dependence and author of *Recover to Live*, recently stated in a CNN interview that drinking at an early age can damage parts of the brain that are still forming, possibly rewiring the brain to crave the substance. This runs somewhat contrary to the thought that allowing kids to drink some at an early age removes part of the mystique, thus possibly minimizing the rampant thrill-seeking binge drinking kids inflict upon themselves once they have enough time away from their parents.

What we do know is this: alcoholism and other chemical dependencies are the Trojan Horses of the family business. When someone is working in a company, especially a publically traded corporation, there is little to no tolerance for alcoholic symptoms. The risk is simply too great. While the danger may be the same in a family business, consequences can be significant.

The vast majority of family business owners believe that the business will remain family owned in the future. Better said, most want the business to be passed on to the next generation. As such, family business owners can tend to overlook, brush off, or even cover up conduct violations that would incur disciplinary action in another company. At the same time, family members can equally let slide a dependency issue with the family business owner.

I encourage you to muster the courage to have the conversation about a known chemical dependency problem in your family business. Yes, it takes some courage and it will be uncomfortable. But there is a lot of good help out there. And your family and business will be the better for it in the long run.

### *When to Let a Family Member Go*

One of the most difficult family business issues to deal with is the poor performance of a family member. The causes can be many, solutions are few, and failure to address it can create not only an underperforming organization, but potentially fracture the family.

Dirty little secret: Entitlement and enablement are the typical culprits. Kids in family businesses grow up seeing their parent leading a group of employees, enjoying some perks in life, and with the ability to take off from work when they want. This environment seduces the next generation into thinking they are also entitled to similar privileges.

Parents, in their zeal to bring their children into the business, or by not being honest with themselves, can overlook their children taking too many liberties. Worse, perhaps they are fully aware of the poor performance but believe the family business is the only way they can make a living. Employees can also be enablers, casting a blind eye, fearing intervention is too risky.

Hardworking siblings also suffer. They want to maintain a good relationship with their underperforming sibling and potential future co-owner. They may bring the issue to the parents, but they will be torn in trying to treat their children equally.

One family business I worked with had kids who arrived late, left early, and surfed the Internet and slept while at work. The father made excuses for them, and they assumed the business would be theirs one day anyhow. Ultimately they were unprepared to lead the business or handle the workload as owners.

Family businesses are notorious for retaining loyal but underperforming employees. However, they are let go when times get tough, and the phrase "should have done that a long time ago" invariably will come out.

Employees who are family members should be treated no differently, but for many owners, relatives are more delicate to handle.

Here are some indicators that members of the next generation are not a good fit to lead:

- They show a lack of initiative, ability and/or desire.

- They are unable to complete tasks.

- They have an abrasive, confrontational, arrogant, or argumentative communication style with employees and clients.

- Their attitude is overly passive or laid back.

- They show an inability to fully grasp the financial elements of the business.

- They make excuses for their poor performance, blaming obligations and interests outside of work.

So, how to proceed? The sooner the situation is addressed, the better. The longer you wait, the more ingrained the family member's belief that poor performance is acceptable, the harder it is to change, and the more likely their feelings will be hurt.

Step one is to be sure the child's other parent is fully apprised of the situation. You do not want to take any action, only to come home and have your spouse exclaim, "How can you do this to our child?" Instead, when the child informs the other parent of their dismissal, the spouse's response should be, "Yes, we have been discussing it all along and we both think this is best for the company and you."

The next step is to lay the groundwork. Perform the same level of due diligence on your child as you would a regular employee. This includes providing training, seeking other areas of the company where they may be more effective, and conducting performance reviews. Most of all, ensure that their managers are not afraid of providing "constructive criticism" about your child. This is harder than you think. Anonymous employee surveys are useful here.

Given that the family member may not be fully aware that his or her performance is lacking, it is important to come prepared: Have a list of instances you are aware of, add in those that other employees may have reported, and if necessary, conduct an anonymous employee survey. Be prepared for excuses and defensiveness.

The next step is to identify the root cause of the issue. It typically comes from one of three places:

- Lack of skill or knack for the particular job.

- Other priorities interfering with performance.

- Lack of interest in the job, and perhaps work altogether.

Perhaps your child is being asked to perform a role he is not very good at. This can be resolved with more training or trying another job. If this has no effect, probe if he has competing priorities. (Typically, you already know). The solution is similar to when there is no motivation – he needs to be pushed and measured to find a way to meet the minimum performance level, or else he needs his responsibilities lowered until he can perform.

Also, be sure to place the situation in context for your child. Running a company is difficult, and no one should feel ashamed of not attaining the top post. Leading a business is an all-encompassing, round-the-clock job, and the ability to run a company differs from other functional skills such as sales or accounting. Perhaps your child's greatest contribution is focusing on what he can do best or where he adds the most value.

I had a client where the dad passed the business on to the accomplished sales director son. But once the son was at the helm, the company headed south. Dad put him back in sales, and the company rebounded.

You also can point to the importance of the business's bottom line as a way to address your child's disappointment over not succeeding dad, or not being as good as a sibling. In reality, the company is the family's "goose that laid the golden eggs," and its success or failure impacts everyone.

The dramatic next-to-last step is to have this child take a week off unpaid to give him time to consider whether this job, work and company is for him. Sometimes they come in Monday and decide it's not. Sometimes they return with resolve. But after you have given your child every chance to succeed in the business, you owe it to him, the family, and the employees to let him go. Here are some words you can use:

*We have tried to find a spot for you here where you can be happy and successful, but it is clear that at this time in your life this work is not a good fit for you. As your boss, I am obligated to let you go. But as your parent, please know that I love you and will do everything I can to help you. My suggestion is that you try to find a vocation that you are truly passionate about. How can I help?*

There will be excuses and even anger. But this is the time for tough love. Don't worry, most times these children find what they were really looking for, or come back years later with the required vigor, maturity, and focus.

## My Interview with Dan Goleman, Author of *Emotional Intelligence*

The book *Emotional Intelligence* articulates that IQ alone, while important, is an inadequate indicator of workplace success. Only when combined with awareness of other's feelings, self-awareness and self-control, the core elements of emotional intelligence, can we predict workplace success.

Dan Goleman's book contains the renowned study of a batch of Harvard graduates and high school valedictorians, and measures their success in the workplace many years later. The clear differentiator was emotional intelligence. For family businesses, a high level of emotional intelligence is vital to the success of the enterprise.

**Henry:** When your book *Emotional Intelligence* first came out in 1995, it was considered a ground-breaking concept and has become standard self-help material ever since. How have your thoughts about EI evolved over the past seventeen years?

**Dan:** My original book discussed the relationship of the brain on emotions, especially as it pertained to children. "How do we help kids?" was the focus. This has now evolved into "What role does EI play in business?" This is centered on competencies such as empathy, managing emotions and social skills. These competencies become especially relevant as individuals reach higher levels of management where they are managing others. My new book on leadership addresses these topics.

### Measuring EI

**Henry:** Is there a "quick and dirty" method of measuring someone's emotional intelligence?

**Dan:** No, but the two best ways are to have 360 feedback from those you work with that is candid and confidential, and to use a simulation where you create a work setting and place people in a high-stress environment. The latter method is, of course, difficult to implement.

In an interview process the best questions will try to elicit a behavior event. For example, "Tell me a time where you did well, and tell me a time where you did poorly." It is the "where you did poorly" answer that is more relevant as it can bring out the degree of the person's self-awareness.

**Henry:** There are people who do not have good EI skills. Is there a way to increase the emotional intelligence of an adult?

**Dan:** Yes. The good news is that EI is learned and can be remedied with individual coaching. Perform a diagnostic on what the key problems are, and then choose one to work on at a time. Create a learning plan. It is just like changing a habit. There must, of course, be buy-in from the participant.

Interestingly, we see that when the behavior has changed that there is a corresponding brain change.

### EI for Family Businesses

**Henry:** What are the Emotional Intelligence issues in a family business?

**Dan:** There are inherent dangers with family businesses. In general, with a family business you have the emotions in a business multiplied by the emotions of a family, plus the hyper-privileged environment that can exist within a family business. This combination can lead to issues.

The purpose of a family is not to pay attention to what is effective, while business is completely geared towards what is effective. Along those lines, there is a propensity to promote family members where needed, even though they may not be capable. The remedy for this is to either build the skills required or find them a different position where their skills are applicable. Overall, it is important that family members be aware of the baggage they are bringing into the business: emotional baggage of the family, and personal emotional baggage. In being aware, it can be managed.

### Beyond EI

**Henry:** Has there been any news with regards to EI?

**Dan:** In a recent interview with Time, I expressed that EI has really become oversold. There are folks out there who have made a cottage industry out of conveying the importance of EI and training people in it. What we need to all understand is that while EI is important, it is not everything. Don't forget that there are other things that are also critical to success, like skills, knowledge and experience.

What an emotionally intelligent thing to say.

In order to spend more time with my kids, Cindy and Jimmy are now on the board!

# CHAPTER 3

## *But What About the Children?*

The wonderful thing about family businesses is that they are *family* businesses. We love our children, we nurture them, educate them, all in the hope that they grow up to be self-sufficient, confident, and happy adults. How nice to be able to work with them also.

Dirty little secret: There is a big difference between working with your children and lining up your succession plan with your kids in mind. I believe there are some basic tenets that can be followed to prepare them to take over the business.

As the owner, you know how to run your business. In operating it successfully for years, you've had to cope with unforeseen events, take risks, and dodge your fair share of bullets. These experiences are stored in your memory databank, which you bring to work every day and leverage as you plan for the day, week, month, and years ahead. Moreover, if you're the second or third generation to run the family business, you also have the information from the earlier generations about running the company.

But the way you think is inherently different from a younger person's point of view. It is impossible for your son or daughter to think and act exactly like you. If you're the founder of the business, this may be even more difficult to keep in mind because it took your entrepreneurial spirit to start the company from scratch, a quality your child may not have.

Interestingly, studies have shown that people we consider to be risk-takers are not thirsty for risk but simply optimistic, determined, and resilient. These characteristics are vital in starting a business. And as the founder of a successful business, it's natural that you would want the same characteristics in your successor. But you would be mistaken in your desire.

This is certainly not to say if your child is a chip off the old block, he cannot succeed. But managing and growing an ongoing concern requires different skills from starting a business. This is exemplified in one respect by looking at the bifurcated business investment world. On the one hand, there is venture capital, where investments are made in starting a new business around an idea. On the other, there is private equity, where investors want to take an ongoing concern and grow it exponentially. These are two different investments with two different business dynamics requiring two different skill sets.

Identifying the unique strengths of your child first requires you to understand that just because he's not exactly like you, it doesn't mean he can't do the job. Along these same lines, and equally important, is patience. Let's say you're a financial wizard, and your child has an inclination in this area, too. Clearly, you're going to be miles ahead of him with all of your experience. Allow him to move at a pace that works for him. Avoid showing off that you know more than he does. Be aware that he will want to do some things on his own. And, most of all, hunt for opportunities to tell him he knows something you didn't or did something that you didn't know how to handle. If he one-upped you, let him know!

Dirty little secret: To start preparing your child for the top position, she must spend some time at the bottom. And I mean on the very bottom. I had a client who was one of the top heating, ventilation and air conditioning, and plumbing companies in the area. The kids all had great potential, but none had spent any time in the field. After discussing with the owners, we decided they needed to begin going out with the crews, getting dirty, digging ditches, working with their hands and understanding the business at the root level. Now they not only understand that part of the business but are respected by all the employees.

The next step is actually quite simple. What do you call someone who is running the entire operation? The "general" manager, because he covers every aspect of the business. How do you prepare someone to become a GM? By having him spend time in each of the key departments. This shouldn't sound like a luxury. Look at yourself. How much of each area do you understand—merchandising, production, management, buying, marketing, financial planning, and the list goes on. Maybe you're not an expert in every area, but you certainly know more than the average bear.

Expose your kids to various aspects of the business. Although not everyone is inclined to be an accountant, sitting behind a desk doing debits and credits will help them understand a core component of the business. Once through all departments, they will not only understand the specific functions but be able to see how they all fit together. At Olan Mills, our family photography business, my first job was to collect and process film canisters. Not thrilling work, but I did get to interface with every department in the company and demonstrate that I was not above doing the dirty work. The next summer I was moved to the office, processing orders.

One of the family business clients I worked with had three potential successors. One is an extroverted people person, another is an introverted analytical type, and the other is in the middle and interested in politics. They're already showing proclivities toward what they ultimately should be doing. But five to ten years from now, they'll each be stronger, and the company will be better off, when each is familiar with every area. When I became involved, we moved each potential successor to jobs that were in line with their skill sets, then a year later we moved them to the area they feared the most. Fortunately, two of the three are in each others' jobs, so they have someone to fall back on. And they are making it.

Now comes the question of education: How much education is enough education? It depends on the type of work the company does, and the type of work your child would like to do there. However, this is the wrong way to look at education. If your children are really attracted to a particular field – even if it's different from the family business – they should pursue it, provided that they know there is a plan for a job in the field after college. Members of the next generation should feel free to explore professions and not feel committed to work for the family business. But if there is some interest in the family business, your children should take courses that align with the company's mission. If they are really interested in the business, they should take a lot of these types of courses.

Once you and your child have found her niche, the key is to stretch her in that area. Another client of mine has an up-and-coming successor who is ultimately headed to the president's chair. She is still young and looking to earn an MBA with a marketing focus, which is good since it's a major element of the business. She has participated in most areas of the operation and heavily in marketing. However, typically marketing doesn't stand alone; it goes along with sales. Currently, she's managing the sales team, but has never actually been in sales. After a conversation with the outside president and founders, we will be proposing she leave the cushy surrounds of the home office and take on the assignment of building a sales territory in a different part of the country.

Now your children have graduated. What now? This is possibly the scariest moment of anyone's life. The regularly scheduled program ends, and there is no predefined plan. You are basically free to do whatever it is that you would like to do, or do nothing at all. The first instinct for many graduates, and even parents of graduates, is to come home and work for the family business. You know you can get hired, you have some experience with the business, and it will enable you to avoid the nightmare of having to look for a job. However, this would be a huge mistake.

When a young person graduates from college, this is the true leaving of the nest and taking flight. And young people should have the opportunity to stretch their wings and find out what they can do and find out who they are. The psychological term is "individuation." One's entire life has been defined as an adjunct to one's parents. Even at college, while some separation occurs and one does have to manage the basic necessities of life, rather little is accomplished in establishing independence.

But once graduation occurs, now is the time to start becoming who you are going to be, or at least begin exploring it. This cannot occur by tucking back under the wing of your parents and the family business. There will certainly be some trial and error, missteps and even mistakes. But there will also be some successes and small victories as well. This is all as it should be in figuring out who are and where your place is in the world.

This brings me to another critical element in the grooming of the next generation's strengths: working with another company. Send them to work somewhere other than the family business. They are young and need to find themselves. They should feel 100 percent free to do whatever they want and work in whatever field they like. That includes relocating to another city, state, or even country. If they are truly intent on joining the family business at some point, they should join a company that has some relation to the business. The son of a prominent family business owner has been going to work for short stints for other similar industry businesses. This is invaluable experience to learn objectively what someone is good at. On top of this, research shows that one of the highest correlations to succession success is the next generation spending some time working outside the business – because now they are their own people, not just dad's kids.

When they rejoin the company, it is preferable that they enter where there is an opening that matches their skills. Or the newbie can enter the company near the bottom for a while to demonstrate that he is learning the basics. Children should be humble and be good listeners. Most of all, they should volunteer to take or lead projects.

To truly determine the next generation's strengths, find out what they like to do. That's the bottom line. If you can find an area they're passionate about or have some strength in, that's where to head. They will view the business from this perspective, whether it's sales, production, or finances. Building upon this strength requires going broader (with outside experience, even in a different industry) and deeper (by creating stretch goals, encouraging outside training, and working with someone who excels in that area).

Finally, while these next-generation members may have been educated in college and had great outside jobs, running a company is complex, so they must always be learning. Encourage your children to attend industry association educational conferences and to read industry and business magazines and books. They should always try to be at the top of their field.

In summary, realize that your children are not you, and your business doesn't require them to be. See that they're well-rounded and encourage them to gravitate to what they enjoy and do best. Actively and passively assist them to excel in that area. Most of all, be patient.

## Summer is an Ideal Time to Get Children Involved in the Family Business

Summer is the time of year when kids are out of school for break, graduating high school and heading off to college, or graduating from college and preparing to face the real world. These are all pivotal moments for children of family business owners. How each stage is handled can have a big impact on the likelihood that the business moves into the next generation.

Summer break is a great time to expose your children to the family business. They can come in as regular employees, get to know some of the employees, and gain an understanding of the business. More importantly, the children can begin to gauge how interested they might be in the business, and you can begin to evaluate whether or not they are really cut out for the family business.

It is pretty hard to go wrong here. But there is one key parameter to success – bring them in at the bottom, just like a summer job for any other kid. Many family business owners go astray by giving their kids more responsibility than they should have or by shielding them from the hard work. If you are in construction, have them go out with the crew. If it is a retail business, let them handle the cash register. If it is an office, let them deal with the paperwork. This is the perfect time for them to realize the base elements of the business.

Everyone grows up going to school, but every May it ends, and we get to reflect on our life journey. While we are young we can explore the family business, but we should also explore the world and how we fit in it.

### *What to Look for in a Mentoring Relationship*

For the potential family business successor, acquiring the requisite education, training and experience to take over the business is critical. Spending time working outside the family business also can be an invaluable experience as it allows the successor to independently discover his or her place in the world unconnected to family. However, the best fine tuning for preparation comes from a good mentoring relationship.

Mentoring is a different animal than just teaching someone how to do the work. It is more about imparting the "secret sauce" on how to look at and approach the business. The focus is to train the person you're mentoring to read between the lines of the business, think strategically about it, and understand what tricks, shortcuts and habits can be successful, and those that will get you into trouble. Learning the nuances of why things went wrong and what could have been done differently can be vastly more instructive than understanding how everything went like clockwork.

Good mentors can be difficult to find. Clearly they need to have spent enough time in business to share their collection of battles won and lost. Mentors also must possess the frame of mind to communicate their knowledge with the goal of grooming their mentees on strategies to approach business and how to prioritize. It is not an opportunity for them to bend an innocent ear or to extol their virtues.

In a family business, there is a ranking of optimal mentors: those outside your family business, but in the industry; outside the family business and out of the industry; inside the family business, but not family; and inside the family business and family. Yes, dad is the worst. This may strike you as odd, but it is simply more difficult for someone who loves you unconditionally to convey hard criticism, and even more difficult for you to hear it. However, sometimes there simply is no choice—maybe your mother or father is the best at what they do.

If you do end up with a parent-child mentoring relationship, the most important thing to remember is that you are not trying to clone the parent. The world and everything in it is evolving. As such, the environment in which your child will be operating will be different and will require actions that are possibly very different than what you had done. Your child needs to be able to take all the knowledge you have imparted, match it to the world he is in, and act accordingly. In addition, people are different. The child has his or her own strengths to bring to bear on the business.

The most important part about a mentor is to have one. Identify who would make a good one and ask. Not only will having a mentor provide you with some business polish, but it will prepare you better for life as well.

## Mentoring Musts You Need to Succeed

Before entering into a mentoring relationship, you and the mentee must agree to commit to the process. Each must understand that there is no defined mentoring step-by-step playbook, but rather a path that will be followed in an effort to raise the mentee's level of understanding of the business and how to influence it.

The road will be bumpy. Mistakes will be made. Everything will not be perfect. You can't expect the mentee to be the perfect sponge to soak up your words of wisdom in just the manner you would like. And the mentee can't expect you to feed him information just the way he wants it, or exactly what he thinks he needs. Be prepared to be patient with your counterpart.

As the mentor, you'll need to let some of your defenses down to convey the most important things the mentee needs to know about the business. Gain his agreement to refrain from judging as you go through the process. In business, as in life, most of the important lessons we learn are not from what we do right, but from what we did wrong. Admitting mistakes and providing all the requisite details so the mentee can understand the nuances of the errors takes a bit of courage. The way the mentee handles this information can facilitate the process.

Be supportive of your mentee. We've all been in situations where the only interaction you have with someone is when something is wrong. That's because when everything is going as expected, there's nothing to be said. But in a learning environment, it is critical to provide encouragement along the way, for two reasons:

1.  The mentee may not be sure if he is doing it right or well, and he needs to know.

2.  If the only thing you hear from someone is criticism, it can become rather discouraging.

Instead of telling your mentee what he is doing wrong, tell him what he should be doing. For example, don't say, "Don't hit the guard rail." Instead try saying, "Stay between the lines." It's still getting the point across, but with a glass-half-full approach. Avoid knee-jerk reactions and the urge to compete, too. We already know you know how to do this with ease, but that's not what this process is about.

Mentoring is about imparting the secret sauce on how to approach the business, helping the mentee learn how to read between the lines of the business and showing him the tricks to making the machine run properly. At the beginning of the relationship, it is vital to reinforce thinking and questioning. A good approach to this is the Socratic Method, i.e., asking questions: "Tell me what you think about that meeting we just had with the sales department. How could it have gone better?" This type of learning process enables you to get into the nooks and crannies of the discussion, and to help the mentee understand the multiple layers of reasoning behind your opinions, as opposed to: "The sales department should have done more of this and less of that."

At the same time, the mentee needs to be comfortable asking "dumb questions." It is mostly through these questions that the mentor can gauge where the mentee is on the learning spectrum.

As with any interaction in the family business, communication is another fundamental element of a successful mentoring process. There needs to be a continual communication process, whether in person or via e-mail or phone. You also need to focus on listening, to ensure you clearly understand where the mentee's mind is at the moment.

This is a good time to discuss the exposure of your communication. While it may be common knowledge that you are mentoring your son, there may be other employees in the business who are envious of this special relationship, which is enabling the mentee to gain insider access behind the scenes of the business. As such, while it can be unavoidable to communicate some things in public, there is no reason to do so in a manner that flaunts the special relationship. Maybe some topics are better discussed one-on-one, behind closed doors.

It is also important, as the mentor, to ensure the mentee is receiving input from more than one source. Line up colleagues who are not in your business to share their thoughts about what it takes to be successful in business or at a particular function. Also, conversations and interactions should take place with other employees who have demonstrated success in certain areas of the company.

Remember that your mentee is not you. He has his own strengths that he needs to bring to bear on the business. Many businesses succeed, not necessarily because they had the right strategy, but because they simply had a person with a rock star skill in a particular area. If you're a great marketer but the mentee is a math whiz, be sure he has a basic understanding of the products and show him the ropes, but let him leverage his natural ability on pricing, purchasing, accounting and financing. (And just to be safe, you may consider hiring a good marketing specialist to help him out!)

## *Tips for Dealing with Children and Wealth in a Family Business*

The nature of a family business is that it is owned by your family. As I have mentioned before, more than 70 percent of all businesses are family businesses. However, as a portion of the workforce, family businesses are clearly on the opposite end of the spectrum. A quick sampling of your neighbors would probably result in the vast majority getting up and going to work in some tech company, an office building downtown, a government office, a medical facility, or one of the many university campuses. My point is that they work for someone else.

This is a wonderful thing. There is a lot of job security in being with a large organization. And for many people, when the small hand hits 5:00 p.m., they can head toward the door. Not so for business owners—if you are not pushing forward every day, then the machine slows down. However, there is also a lot more control that comes with being a business owner, and by definition, you are in charge of everything and everyone. And all the profit goes to the owners.

The contrast between business owners and nonbusiness owners can skew the perspective of life of the children of those business owners. Especially if there is some significant wealth involved.

There is a famous saying, "Shirtsleeves to shirtsleeves in three generations." Basically, someone starts a business, the next generation makes it a success, and then the third wrecks it. Why? Because they became disconnected from understanding the hard work required to run the business and felt that there was so much money coming in that there was no need to work hard. You could simply live a life of leisure. Interestingly, there is a similar saying in many countries around the world: "clogs to clogs," "rice paddy to rice paddy," etc.

Few people could be more attuned to this dynamic than Warren Buffett. As such, he stars in an animated series called *The Secret Millionaires Club*. The purpose of the series is to help kids understand money and develop healthy habits from a young age.

Reflecting on the saying that "The chains of habit are too light to be felt until they're too heavy to be broken," Buffett says, "We're trying to help kids develop healthy habits that will help them their whole life. It's never too early. Whether it's teaching kids the value of a dollar, the difference between needs and wants, or the value of saving, these are all concepts that kids encounter at a very early age, so best to help them to understand it."

One of the great lessons that can be learned within a family business is teaching the next generation the value of work, saving money and reinvesting for the future. It's much more valuable to teach children how to fish than to give them the fish. Very few family businesses perpetuate into the next generation without learning this key lesson. Parents know full well that they are setting the example for their kids by their actions. For family business owners, it counts double. It is so easy to create a more comfortable ride for your child, pick her up after a mistake or ensure she avoids it in the first place. And it can be very alluring to use money to fix her problems.

But the most valuable dollar a child will ever get is the one she earned on her own merit. And the greatest accomplishment comes from trying, failing, persevering and succeeding. That is how you break the cycle of shirtsleeves to shirtsleeves in three generations.

## Fighting Entitlement with a Dose of Reality: Protecting Kids from Hardship and Failure Robs Them of Resilience

It's no secret that entitlement is a huge problem in the next generation of high-net-worth families and family businesses. The wealth-creator generation worked so hard to build something, often from nothing. Understandably, they may want to protect the next generation from all the hardship they entailed. But that is one of the main causes of the "shirtsleeves to shirtsleeves in three generations" problem. Protecting children from hardships is a huge mistake, because the ups and downs, setbacks and failures are where the parents developed their resilience and the very skills it took to "fail their way to success."

Telling "war stories" over the dinner table or at family gatherings is a great way to pass down lessons learned from even the most embarrassing moments in the family business history. The fact that the family overcame these difficulties puts a heroic spin on the story. One idea may be to halt the telling at the critical arc of the story, and ask the children how they might have solved the problem. Then reveal what you actually did and how things resolved.

There are many opportunities parents miss to teach children about wealth creation, the value, pride and fun of hard work, and the importance of being frugal no matter how much money one has. For instance, instead of driving home with a shiny new car, why not take the children, ages 10 and up, to the dealer so they can experience test driving different cars and sitting down with the dealer while you haggle over the price and terms? It's a great way for them to learn about the process of purchasing a car — including the parents' style of negotiating, their values about safety, efficiency and other automotive issues.

My favorite antidote to entitlement is philanthropy. Collect solicitations that come in the mail and sift through them together every few months to vote on which ones most resonate. You can even draw up some criteria such as x percent for global vs. local; environmental vs. health or specific diseases that have impacted family or friends; animals vs. the latest natural disaster, etc. You can show your kids how to look up on the Internet how well each organization is managed, in terms of how much of its funds actually are spent on the cause versus administrative and marketing expenses.

Volunteering at the local soup kitchen, nursing home or 5K run for various causes is a great way to do good while strengthening family bonds.

The point is to keep talking, and keep listening. In fact, the main factor researchers found that correlates with teens and at-risk behaviors such as drug or alcohol abuse, pregnancy, crime and dropping out of high school, was whether or not parents are home for dinner a few nights a week. If that seems too simple, think again. It really, truly is just about showing up, and keeping the dialog going.

Jayne A. Pearl, coauthor (with Richard A. Morris) of *Kids, Wealth, and Consequences: Ensuring a Responsible Financial Future for the Next Generation*
http://www.kidswealthandconsequences.com

# SECTION III

*Business*

# CHAPTER 4

## Money Matters for a Family Business

Some family businesses succeed. Some fizzle out. Others go out with a loud bang. We have all heard of the family businesses that didn't make it. Something went wrong--trust broke down, relationships started to fracture, and in the worst case, lawsuits broke out. There are a variety of possible reasons why, but one of the typical reasons is money.

Dirty little secret: When money is involved some people's behavior can go sideways. When there is a lot of money, some people turn into Mr. Hyde. Sadly, money is a big contributor to family business failures, broken families, and unhappy Thanksgivings.

What is the most important action a family business can take? Installing appropriate governance. That means having a board of advisers with some members who are not family or friends. Pay should be based on position and contribution. Bringing in a nonfamily leader sometimes is the right answer. There is a difference between being a good owner and a good manager.

### *Tips on Dealing with Money in a Family Business*

To be sure, money can be very seductive. Those who work with family businesses know the power money can have in ripping apart a family business. Money is certainly beneficial in life, but only to a point. At the bottom end of Maslow's famous hierarchy of needs, money can buy you a lot of food, shelter, and security. But moving up the scale, not only does money become less important, it can be a hindrance to developing true love, self-esteem, and self-actualization.

So what happens with these family businesses? Where do they go wrong, and what can be done? The best action that a family business can take to ensure the longevity of the business is to have a board with some independent representation. Most all highly functioning and multigeneration family businesses have a board, and have folks on it who are qualified and have no conflict of interest. When issues arise, money or otherwise, a good unbiased opinion can get people back on track.

Compensation is also a tricky area. Many family business owners have a hard time paying their family members actual market value. Gifts and kind-hearted parental assistance get mixed up with salary. And then keeping equality among the children gets trickier. If the compensation does not end up out of whack for some members, then it ends up out of alignment in the other direction when everyone is paid the same, regardless of their role and contribution.

Then, once the parents are gone, the children are left with an unfair compensation system and the burden of trying to get it straight. Try to keep a good relationship with your brother, who is a lower level employee, after you've had to cut his pay – not an easy thing to do.

Another mistake parents make is that in order to keep peace among their children, they remain at the helm much longer than they should. This results in poor communication with no one discussing the real issues. Hence, once mom and dad are gone, a battle for control ensues. Without the habit of good communication, legal action can result.

What makes matters worse is if the company is making significant profit, but there are few other assets outside the business. This forces the other siblings who might otherwise leave the business to be forced to stay in and fight for their "fair share." Having life insurance can help here.

Finally, when there is significant wealth involved, prepare your kids. Teach them to differentiate between wants and needs, the benefits of delayed gratification, and that sometimes the answer is no. Make sure they have had a real job doing real work, understand saving and investing, and the importance of charitable giving – physical and monetary.

**Psychology of Money**

Ted Klontz, Ph.D., specializes in the effects money has on the psyche. At his presentations he asks a few folks to count a stack of one dollar bills. Afterward he informs them that the mere act of counting money increases the level of oxytocin in the body – the "feel good hormone." Conversely, he will stand in front of the audience, whip out a $20 bill, say "Watch this," and proceed to tear it in half. The audience is always shocked, with some people gasping. (Note: It is a fake $20.) His point is to demonstrate people actually feel physical pain when seeing money destroyed.

### *Your Family Business is Not the Family Cash Register*
Family businesses face a variety of challenges that "normal" businesses do not have to deal with. Clearly the relationships between the

family members who are working in the business, and even those who are not, create a different dynamic. One issue in particular is how to manage the money.

When you are in a family business, there is an inherent level of trust that exists. Mom, dad, son, and daughter are all happily working to drive the business forward.

Dirty little secret: Often when everyone has an ownership mentality, each believes he or she uses and spends company funds as he or she sees fit--sometimes even for personal benefit.

I knew a family business with a married couple and two children working in the business. Everyone had corporate credit cards, and the parents had checkbooks on top of that. The daughter was spending money to drive marketing, the son was using funds on manufacturing, and the dad was using the company funds as his own personal piggy bank.

The good news is that the company was doing so well that it didn't matter, until there was a downturn. Then there was yelling, finger pointing, and general chaos.

The opposite can also occur: "We manage our finances very tightly," says Sally Crowell, president of Crowell Systems, a software provider to health care providers. "Our daughter has a background in accounting, and we run everything through her. Moreover, all of our systems come with financial management software for our customers, so we practice what we preach."

It is easy to see how an environment where everyone feels they are entitled to access the bank account can be problematic. Here are five pointers to stave off problems before they crop up:

- Have some financial policies. Who has access to the checkbook? Who has access to cash? How are expenditures recorded? What are the spending limits? What is personal versus business spending?

- Have a budget. If you are a larger company, this is not an issue, but many small companies shy away from the idea of a budget as they fear how complicated it can be. But at the most basic level, it does not have to be. The simplest budget is to take last year's income statement, look at the percent of revenue spent in each of the expense categories, and if it was a decent year, establish those percentages as targets for the next year. Taking it a step further, if you are aware of any new, big, or unusual expenditures that will need to occur in the coming year, declare them now. Don't wait until the money is needed, or spend it and inform everyone later.

- Set specific dates and times on the calendar to conduct formal monthly meetings to review the financial statements, measure your progress and ensure all are informed.

- Have a single point of contact to manage the finances. If you are small enough you can rely on a family member. If not, you will need to bring in someone from the outside. You will cringe at the price tag that goes along with a qualified accountant. But the difference between a good accountant and a bad one is the difference between knowing exactly where you are in the business, proactively driving it and pursuing tax advantages, and basically trying to drive your car with thick mud covering your entire windshield--you can't see, and it is hard to clean up.

- Have a good external CPA who can review your books once a quarter to ensure that everything is in order.

Not having financial policies and procedures established for the family business can lead to poor spending habits, misunderstandings and lack of trust. But instilling good financial discipline leads to better business performance and a healthy family environment.

### *Proceed With Caution: Compensation Issues Can Be Sticky*

Compensation in the family business is one of the trickiest areas to address: How much should the kids make? How about when you are siblings? If dad is starting to spend less time at work, what should his compensation be? For those who feel they are unfairly compensated, how do you bring up the topic without seeming to be greedy and selfish?

Dirty little secret: One of the pitfalls in family business lies in compensation. It's deeper than just money. People view salary as a gauge, rightly or wrongly, of not only their worth to a company, but of how successful they are in life. To continue the legacy, business owners often offer more to the second generation than is feasible.

In one family business I know, the son has been plugging away trying to drive the business forward. He has taken over the leadership role but does not have any shares in the company. Since the performance of the company, and the industry as a whole, has been under extreme pressure, he has not had a raise in quite some time. However, the situation is becoming awkward: He is now in the position to be able to work elsewhere for substantially more income than he is earning now. And since he does not have any equity ownership, if his parents were to die today, he would simply receive his pro rata portion of the estate. (In the meantime, his other siblings work elsewhere and garner much higher wages.)

In another family business the son is the top administrator and, regardless of evaluations, raises have ended. There is a feeling that he is already at the top of the income bracket for his position. In yet another family business, there are up-and-coming company leaders, but they are still quite young. They are feeling they deserve a higher wage.

Unfortunately there is no one single answer for compensation within the family business. But there are some rules of thumb: Try to establish an open understanding of how compensation will be dealt with. Be open about what factors are important in determining the total compensation.

Determine as best you can what market value is for the position. This can be acquired through an HR professional, but a rough idea can be found through a salary calculator or contacting friends at similar companies.

There is also a tendency to feel the fair thing to do is pay each child working for the business equally. There was a family business that had four children, each 25 percent owners, where each were paid the exact same salary. This seemed odd, as they all had very different levels of responsibility. Clearly, those in executive positions should be compensated at a higher level than a drafting person or a salesperson. This situation created enormous tension, and it came about because the parents didn't want to deal with the emotions that come from having to explain to one child why they don't make as much money as his or her sibling. Remember that the fair thing is to pay employees the appropriate salary for the work they are doing.

Avoid the temptation to overpay. It sets a bad precedent, is difficult to reverse, and is impossible to explain to nonfamily employees who may be more deserving. It's easy to see how family businesses can slide into compensation problems if dad is trying to lure children into the business by overpaying them. It makes sense that if junior is getting paid more at the family business than elsewhere, he'll stay long enough, and it will eventually grow on him.

Here's the issue: As my professor Bob Bontempo at Columbia Business School told us many years ago, the key to negotiating a salary is your starting salary. Every year, you will get a raise, and with compounded interest over time, you can be making serious money. It all depends on how high you start.

Once you've overpaid the kids to start in the business, years may pass before you realize they're getting paid more than they should. How do you explain that their raise will be so low? Then, when the next child comes into the business, you are forced to treat them the same way as their sibling, otherwise you will have some explaining to do. The bottom line is resist the temptation to buy your kids into the business.

The best answer is to communicate the situation to them from the beginning:

*Son/Daughter, this is a business, and I own it. I would love for you to be a part of it. There are many benefits to owning and running your own business. There are also downsides. At the end of the day, when I pass away, the business will belong to you and your siblings. In the meantime, it's a machine that generates money for the family. We must all ensure that the machine is working well. If you have interest and skill, then you could be a part of the business. However, it's important to understand that it needs to be a professional relationship. The business will pay you what you are worth to the business.*

*As you become more valuable to the business, it will pay you more. It's possible that one day you may run and own the business, but that's only if you are the best one to run it. You have brothers and sisters. They are welcome to join the business if there's a need, and they have interest and some skill. It's important to understand that all the kids will be paid differently, just as any group of employees is paid differently.*

They need to understand that because they are your children, they will eventually be owners of the business, whether they join the business or not. If they aren't in the business, the business would be sold. But if they have an interest in continuing the business, here's their chance.

If there is insufficient cash for appropriate salaries, you can consider providing some equity. Owners can be overly gun-shy about giving equity. As a family business it is important to understand that minority ownership creates little to no say about the operations of a business. Thus there is no loss of control. However, it does provide a sense of ownership on behalf of the recipient. Moreover, it is an excellent estate planning mechanism.

Now, with all of this said, when the company makes a profit, the owners can retain that profit for their own desires. And just as any family would do, parents can give financial gifts to their children. The IRS has an annual exclusion limit for how much gift money can be given before it must be taxed as income. And I am not suggesting you should not "optimize" your tax burden. But it should be made clear that this money has nothing to do with being in the business and should not be confused with pay for performance at work.

Finally, as always, the most important part of any family business compensation situation is communication. On an ongoing basis, the best way to handle compensation is to not handle it. Have a high-level manager determine salaries, get the advice of an HR professional or simply look on one of many salary sites to gauge what an appropriate salary would be. But if you plan to manage it yourself, do it offsite, and allow for enough time to talk it through. Don't discuss numbers, but discuss what each feels is relevant to earning compensation, and what is not. Money is always an awkward topic, especially when discussing how much I should get and how much you should get. But guessing at compensation without an open understanding of what factors contribute to it can create a misunderstanding, suspicion, and animosity. An outside facilitator can help.

*Negotiating Shareholder Agreements: What You Need to Know*

When it comes to making decisions for your business, the overriding issue is who gets the most say in answering questions that arise. We all think the person with the most ownership should, since the majority owner has greater control and more say than the minority shareholders. However, in the case of multiple shareholders with equal share portions, the group needs to come together as a majority to determine control of the company.

Consider putting into place a shareholder agreement: "an arrangement among a company's shareholders describing how the company should be operated and the shareholders' rights and obligations," as described by Investopedia. It not only outlines the parameters of operations and the rights of shareholders, it also includes information on the regulation of the shareholders' relationship, the management of the company, ownership of shares and the privileges and protection of shareholders. It helps ensure shareholders are treated fairly and their rights are protected. The agreement outlines the fair and legitimate pricing of shares, particularly when sold. It also allows shareholders to decide what outside parties may become future shareholders, and provides safeguards for minority positions.

## Buy-Sell Agreements

One of the main components to any shareholder agreement is the buy-sell agreement. A buy-sell agreement is a contract between the co-owners of the business to buy or sell their respective interests under certain situations, such as the death or retirement of an owner or simply the desire to cash out. The pricing and payment methodology is also usually spelled out.

While this may seem straightforward, that's not always the case, and it can get even messier in a family business. With a family business that has been passed down through multiple generations, there can be radically differing interests and backgrounds.

I had a second-generation family business client where there were three brothers running the business. There was a significant difference of opinion among the oldest brother and the middle brother on the definition of work - the oldest had a more puritan work ethic, while the middle one's view was "bohemian." Needless to say, the middle brother was pushed out. While they are brothers and do love each other, working through the details of what constituted "fair" in terms of a buy-out was awkward and uncomfortable.

The older one, who was the president and was tiring, had fewer financial obligations. The youngest one was eight years his junior, not the president but a diligent worker and married. Once the middle brother departed, the two remaining brothers decided to put an agreement in place to guard against any unforeseen eventualities. And so the shareholder agreement and buy-sell agreement came into play.

## Key Questions to Ask

The first reaction in considering a shareholder agreement is to engage with an attorney, but the true first step is to engage in multiple discussions, over time, about what can be referred to as the "touchy-feely" issues. The parties in the agreement need to understand the personal and professional goals of each of the family members.

The ultimate goal is that—with a truly comprehensive understanding of each other's situation, whether you agree with it or not—everyone can move forward together. There also needs to be a good comprehension of the intrinsic financial life of the business as it passes from one generation to the next.

Some key considerations that always need to be negotiated when it comes to a shareholder agreement or buy-sell in a family business:

- Do you need to work at the company to own shares of it? While this keeps control in the hands of those who know the company best, there may be insufficient liquidity to buy out those who leave.

- Do you want to be in business with your in-laws? What if they know nothing about the business? What if they are really good?

- How do you value the company? It can be valued by a certified valuation professional at the time of an event, or you can agree on book value for the sake of the business.

- Where will the money come from for a buy-out? In the case of a death, life insurance. Predetermine a plan that will not materially damage the company if someone decides they want to leave and needs the money, which is usually a payout over multiple years.

Remember, the important thing in figuring out how to negotiate a shareholder agreement or a buy-sell is establishing them before you ever need them.

## Make Giving a Part of Your Family Business

From a tax-planning perspective, philanthropy can certainly be advantageous. As Steve Watt, director of planned gifts at North Carolina State University (the largest university in the state) puts it, "Assets can be donated to a charity such that capital gains are avoided and you get a tax deduction."

Watt explained that you also receive the income from the assets during your lifetime, and can establish your life insurance in such a way that your children will receive an inheritance equivalent to the original asset value. Through this, the charity receives the value of the original asset – and you may avoid some estate taxes. (Now you understand why your alma mater is always knocking on your door.)

However, from an emotional and psychological perspective, much more is going on.

Family businesses are breeding grounds for entitlement. Companies that are reasonably successful can generate some impressive income. As a result, owners may splurge on items they couldn't afford when they were growing up – on themselves, and on their children.

This unbridled spending can have a negative effect on children's perspective of money. While certainly nothing can substitute for developing a good work ethic at a young age, witnessing philanthropic giving by a parent can have a very positive impact on one's attitude toward money.

Growing up with a lot of money, without appropriate measures being taken, can result in children who have uncontrolled spending habits, with their identities wrapped up in money. There's also the risk of them having a lack of ambition, and – worst of all – a lack of self-esteem.

To be sure, philanthropic giving cannot rectify poor parenting. However, watching your role models donate money to good causes for no other reason than that they believe in helping those in need or promoting a good cause, and truly not wanting or expecting anything in return, puts a healthy stake in the ground on the purpose of money.

My mother donated money to a school that only accepted children who were growing up in poverty, with the mission of teaching students self-reliance. This always had an effect on me.

Having a parent die is incredibly sad. That unconditional love and support you have always had is now gone. Parents serve as a cohesive element: They keep the family together, even though it may be spread out, have different lives, and even contain some conflict. Once this focal point is no longer there, it becomes very difficult for the family to stay connected.

Philanthropic giving, especially some sort of trust, where the children must come together to make decisions, can provide a vehicle to keep the family connected over time. While it can be anything, setting up something that the family remembers you for can be special. No, it will not reconcile family differences. But it does somewhat obligate everyone to come together, if just for a day, for a positive purpose, and remember the good times. It's kind of like Thanksgiving.

### Know When to 'Go Pro' with Your Family Business

Perhaps your brother, the company finance guru, has sloppy bookkeeping habits. Or your daughter, in charge of sorting inventory during slow stretches at your retail shop, instead checks Facebook while on the clock. And you can't even remember the last time you all had a team meeting to discuss how business is going.

Think long and hard about how your business came to be. Your family business didn't start as a family business. It began from someone simply trying to generate an income. Perhaps someone experienced a flash of insight into a hot market opportunity. Or maybe someone just stumbled onto something big.

A client of mine declared, "I never thought I would be in business with my kids. I was simply trying to build something that would generate enough money for us all to live on. And then it snowballed." As they are in the assisted living business – and baby boomers are heading their way en masse – they are sitting pretty.

But the founders of that business, and other successful ones, had to possess essential traits during their startup phase:

- A certain level of smarts

- The willingness and ability to work extremely hard

- A decent business idea

- Initiative to act on luck that came their way

- An ability to take creative and persistent approaches to problem solving

Now let's take that business and fast-forward twenty years. Add on millions of dollars in revenue, and a lot more employees. Reactionary management, no matter how adroit, will no longer suffice.

I know a family business that had become a national brand, with sales across the United States and their own manufacturing facility. But the founders still ran things off-the-cuff: meetings were ad hoc, employees were hired and fired on a whim, and financial management meant seeing how much money was in the bank. Showing leadership meant fighting the hottest fire of the day.

Things had to change if they were to survive. That's because when the next generation becomes involved in the family business, they adopt the management methods they see. Their response for doing so is typically, "That's the way dad always did it." However, once the business gets to a certain size, management by the seat of your pants is no longer sufficient. The business must professionalize in order to survive and make it to the next level. The focus must change from working *in* the business to working *on* the business.

Here are some tried and true tips to professionalizing your family business:

- Hire only the most qualified people for jobs. This could mean bringing in some nonfamily professionals – one of the major recommendations of a recent PwC Family Business Survey according to Margaret Young, the Private Practice Managing Partner.

- Use formal evaluation systems.

- Base your pay system on market rates for the position. Resist paying high salaries just because they are family.

- Conduct regular reviews of your financial data.

- Hold meetings, and take a disciplined approach to them.

- Assemble a board of advisors. Include members who are not involved in your family business.

- Adopt a philosophy of good communication and transparency.

Many family businesses fear professionalizing the business because flexibility may be reduced, the "family feel" might diminish, and it will just not be as much fun. However, gradually implementing elements of professional management over time will reduce chaos, improve accountability, and most of all improve business results. And a better bottom line is always fun.

## Unique Estate Planning Tool for Those who are "ABIL"

Family business owners spend a lifetime building something special and of value many times only to have to fire sale all or part of it to pay taxes, possibly leaving less than 15 percent of your current wealth after taxes. At the same time, some owners buy life insurance using their own liquid assets to pay for life premiums, often triggering gift taxes and always incurring a significant opportunity cost. And many times the return on investment is only positive if the insured dies early, not an attractive option.

However, there is a unique financing tool available to some family business owners called ABIL or "Asset Backed Insurance Lending." These transactions allow business owners or those with significant wealth to address their tax liability without having to liquidate the very assets they have spent a lifetime building. It enables you to control what is done with your assets when you pass on, without having the government decide for you. ABIL is about doing the planning and minimizing the cost while keeping control of most, if not all, of your assets.

Source: Grace Barnard, President of NIW Companies
http://www.niwcorp.com/

Kids, someday all this will be yours — unless we can find someone else.

# CHAPTER 5

# *It's Time to get Your Contingency Plans in Order*

Cameron Evans, a wealth strategist and vice president at First Citizens Bank, starts his conversations with potential clients with this simple question: "What would happen to your family, your business and your wealth if you were to die right in the middle of this sentence?" While this may sound harsh, the family business owner or patriarch can only speculate what might happen.

Another method to get at the heart of this issue is to conduct a "fire drill" - scheduling a mandatory conference call one morning from home, with no subject, and inviting all family members in the business and key managers to participate. Once everyone is gathered around, wondering what's going on, you would tell them you are perfectly fine, but you want them to spend the day pretending you just had a heart attack and died. Instruct them to react accordingly and be prepared to discuss this the following morning. The following morning, you will probably find that there are more questions than answers.

So what are some steps that can be taken now in order to ensure your business continues to operate smoothly even when it has just lost its leader?

## *Opening the Discussion*

A colleague of mine informed me of a family business that experienced a tragedy: the founder and true heart and soul of the business had suddenly died of a heart attack at the age of 53. He had three children, all working in the business, and each was married, with each spouse also working in the business. Mom, however, did not and had not ever worked in the business - and she was now the new owner of the business. When the kids came to her looking for instructions, she had none. When asked if dad had told her what do if this were to ever happen, she had no answers, at which point the children and spouses all began implementing their individual strategies to influence mom to enact their opinion of the best course of action. You can imagine the family discord that ensued, and you can imagine what happened to the business.

What could have been done? Dad could have taken mom aside and told her his wishes, were he to die. This is certainly the bare minimum. A better plan would be to call a family meeting and, at least, declare his wishes. Even better would be to actually open the question up to discussion so the entire family could weigh in on the best course of action.

The best course of action would be to enlist the assistance of a good family business consultant or estate planning attorney to guide you. Yes, this will cost money, but these folks specialize in helping people work through these questions and, more importantly, have seen the successes and failures of other family businesses working through these same issues. A good advisor will work with you to understand your wishes, and will then gather the key stakeholders together to ensure they are informed as well.

What about when it comes to preparing the next generation? You may have your eye on a specific family member to take over your business or simply run an important part of it. What would happen if he were unable to come to work one day due to a tragedy - or simply not wanting the job anymore?

One common method is to constantly focus on training and cross-training. It can be tempting to want to go on your own to accomplish tasks or run a department. However, what would happen if the heir apparent was simply out sick for a week with the flu? Do you have sufficiently trained support to cover while he's out? Maybe it's not just one person as backup, but a small group that can be put in place to cover. This clearly cannot substitute for someone if he is gone for good, but at least there is a safety net in place. And, just as any smart businessperson would cross-train staff over time to reduce the reliance on certain people in key roles, cross-training others to understand even the basics can go a long way.

One common error many family businesses make is to ignore family members who are not in the business. One of my clients had a situation where the heir apparent son, through a process of soul-searching, had come to the realization that he didn't want to run the company. He wanted to focus on other things in life. While meeting with the business owners' daughter, who was highly successful at a different company in a different city, I asked her opinion about the future of the family business. She declared that she was the best solution to the problem. But her parents never thought to ask her if she was interested in leaving her current job to come back to the family business.

In this case, the job the daughter had was similar to that of the family business. However, this does not always have to be the case. Sometimes family members can come in from completely different areas and be effective, as long as they have the requisite ability and desire to perform.

I'm not telling you to drag your kids into the business and everything will be fine, but I am saying that if you have lost a key next generation family member in the business, don't completely ignore what other family members might bring.

## *Creating an Advisory Board*

One of the most important steps a family business can take when preparing a succession plan is to instill a healthy level of governance, including policies, procedures and a board of directors. Many smaller family businesses think they're too small for a board. Dirty little secret: They are wrong. This misperception comes mostly from their belief that the word "board" means "board of directors," which means individuals elected by a corporation's shareholders to oversee the management of the corporation. The members of a board of directors are paid in cash and/or stock, meet several times each year and assume legal responsibility for corporate activities.

The keywords here are "legal responsibility." To get a qualified individual to take on legal responsibility for a small- to medium-sized business can be rather difficult. Thus, smaller family businesses would be correct in saying they're too small for a board of directors. This is why they would form a board of *advisors*—it is exactly the same, without legal responsibilities, and as such, is much easier to form.

There are many benefits to having a board of advisors. You can staff it with individuals who have knowledge and background in some of the key areas your company focuses on or would like to move into. This is most important with any board: Put independent-minded people on it, not your golfing buddy who ran a company or your cousin who is a sales whiz. You need a group of folks who are each willing and able to give you honest feedback without fear of reprisal. Once in place, this group begins to act like a fine wine—it gets better with age, providing a long term sense of continuity.

For example, the CEO of a multi-generation family business with a prominent brand product has an advisory board of three trusted professionals. They meet three or four times a year for a long lunch, during which the CEO gives an update, highlights important issues, gets some feedback, and goes on his way. This method works well for them and maybe it would for you, too.

If your heir apparent were to fall seriously ill or die, it would be a personal and business tragedy. A good advisory board can play an invaluable role in assisting your company through this difficult time. While your family is grieving, the advisory board could engage in the business temporarily to hold down the fort, and it could consider the best options for the business going forward.

Certainly, the board is not a silver bullet, but it can act as a wonderful safety net if things go wrong in the family business.

## *Dealing with Death in a Family Business Poses Unique Challenges*

Though it is something most of us would rather not think about, death is an issue that cannot be ignored in a family business, especially because of how suddenly it can strike and the breadth of its impact.

In my years of consulting to family businesses I have only experienced death in a family business two times. While neither was a surprise, one did alter the course of the family business. It was a second-generation family business with two brothers working together, with the third generation employed and striving to make its mark, when the mother and cofounder died. She had put up a good fight against cancer, but at some point it was time to concede, and just a few weeks later she passed away.

It was not unexpected. All the affairs were in order, travel plans had been postponed, goodbyes had been said, and all had steeled themselves against the oncoming wave of past memories, good and bad, and the emotional sadness that inevitably follows. While everyone grieves in his or her own way, there was an acknowledgement that the show must go on when it comes to the family business. At least for a while.

As time wore on, the perspective of the remaining family members subtly began to change. While the two brothers had already assumed full control of the company, there was awareness that now they were truly on their own. They had been trained, the business has been transitioned, and yes, they were now in charge. But the door to the house had always been open to stop by for a hot cup of coffee and a good conversation about whatever was on their mind. No more.

It was a sense that their release valve/security blanket was now gone, and they now had to assume the top spot in the pecking order previously held by mom. Two things began to happen: A more serious focus ensued as to "What do I want to do with the rest of my life, and how does that fit with my role in the business?" and a realization dawned that the volume had been turned up on preparing for and figuring out the succession plan for the next generation.

At the same time, the next generation had become cognizant that the time had arrived for them to step up their leadership role in the business if they were to assume control of the business one day. And if not, perhaps they needed to seek their life's ambition outside the family business.

As an adviser to the family business, my role was quite delicate in this situation. No logic, knowledge, or business savvy in the world could have any influence on the emotional situation that this was. Certainly time must be allocated for the grieving process, and issues that were previously on the front burner must be slowly eased back into. But similar to the life perspective change that happens to you when you bring a new life into the world, a perspective change comes about when the one who brought you into the world leaves. The issues that were hot before really didn't seem so important anymore.

## Solving Family Business Issues Takes Time

I am frequently asked what it is that I do when I try to help family businesses. This is a difficult question to answer, as no family or business situation is like another – the players are different, and each has his or her unique hopes, dreams, and desires. Moreover, the uniqueness of the family, with its unquestioning love, is intermingled with the business which is trying to make a profit and run efficiently.

It is really half psychology and half business. So when people ask me how to fix a family business, I often declare that it can be similar to a psychologist: They can't necessarily tell you what's wrong, but they can take you through a process to help you figure out what you want to do and how to get there. (Sorry, there is no app available to address your family business issues.)

But let me share one best practice with you. Success in business is pretty simple: Do it better, faster, and cheaper than your competition, and you will win (assuming there is a modicum of market out there). However, this approach does not always work well inside the family business. Sometimes slower is better when trying to make certain changes in the family business.

I had a client where there were a number of equal owners involved. The discussion revolved around the transitioning out of the long-time leader, the process to determine the new leader and the governance rules that would be used going forward. The meeting took quite some time and there was a lot of discussion.

I asked awkward and sometimes uncomfortable questions to ensure all the issues got out on the table. In the end everyone came to an agreement on the timing, the process, and the governance structure.

There was no yelling, and no punches were thrown – just a lot of good honest discussion.

Later, when I was debriefing with one of the equity owners, he expressed his frustration with the meeting: "I think we could have done the whole thing in 15 minutes and gotten back to work."

The owner of another family business had a similar attitude. We had covered a lot of material and had done some really good work over a few days. But there was an important issue that we had not had time to get into so far – family compensation.

The owner was a hard-driving business person, focusing on the details and letting the big picture take care of itself. Speed was of the essence – whenever there is an issue, let's get it addressed and move on. This perspective paid off in spades for the business over the years. So when he suggested we quickly gather the kids into a room and hammer this out in an hour before I left and he was about to go out of town, I demurred.

His kids had been working in the business for quite some time. But the structure of the salaries had gotten out of control. Elements of compensation were ambiguous, and some benefits had been hastily put into place. It was clear that in order to get the entire compensation package for the family members back into some kind of line, there were going to be disagreements. And some were going to walk away with less than what they originally had.

The better answer was to wait until everyone could spend the time required to fully discuss the topic, get all the data on the table, state desires and rationales, and forge a solution in which all parties could gain an understanding of what was being done, if not come away completely satisfied. This is what was done, and the end result was a sensible compensation program that made sense and everyone bought into.

Dirty little secret: Business is logic and family is emotion. When dealing with family on a business topic, especially if it is personal, be sure to allocate sufficient time. If you cut it short, you will end up with a solution that is not supported – and with hurt feelings. How much time? As much as it takes.

## Do You Need Help?

As a consultant to family businesses I am frequently asked, "What is a family business consultant?" The simple answer is that when you need one, you will know it! But allow me to shed more light on the topic.

A consultant is brought in to help you solve a particular problem that you either don't have the time or expertise to solve yourself. There are basically two kinds of consultants:

1.  Expert consultants give you solutions to particular problems and/or implement those solutions.

2.  Process consultants help you define the problems and assist you in reaching your own conclusion and course of action.

So what should you be looking for in a good consultant? The first and most important factor is straightforward – Can this consultant solve your problem?

Here is the five-step litmus test: How much experience does he or she have solving this type of problem? How broad and deep is this consultant's training? Does he or she have any actual business? Does this person actively demonstrate subject matter expertise and thought leadership? Has this consultant successfully helped other businesses with this problem?

Some people get hung up on understanding the approach or process. I put this as a secondary consideration. Business history is littered with poor implementations of good models. If you can solve my problem, I don't particularly care how.

Two other basic criteria are cost and time. Can you afford it, and if there is a time constraint, can the consultant complete the project on time? No doubt, these are important factors, but you should first be sure this consultant can solve your issue. A quick and cheap solution that doesn't solve your problem is not very useful!

Family business consultants are a unique breed as they help clients work through a broad range of intertwined issues, with the consequence of failure being the loss of not only the business, but also the love found in family relationships. While the multifaceted issue of succession is foremost, there are ownership concerns, communication and conflict issues, and ongoing governance needs.

Moreover, family businesses are incredibly complex entities as they inherently combine three nonrelated elements: a family with a business with ownership. The success factors of each are completely different but must all coexist in harmony.

Thus, there are many skills sets that come into play in assisting a family business, the two critical ones being the ability to deal with the family element and the business element. It is a combination of the expert consultant and the process consultant. Other areas include knowledge of law, tax, insurance, finance, etc.

Just as an attorney must pass the bar or an accountant must become certified, family business consultants become certified through the global governing body FFI, the Family Firm Institute, as Certified Family Business Advisors (CFBA). Running a business is hard, especially these days. Trying to run a profitable business with your family and maintain family harmony is extra difficult. Fortunately there is help available for all of it.

Dirty little secret: Getting help helps. A family business owner has spent his life dedicated to successfully running his business, not learning the intricacies of family business succession. Bringing in any kind of help inherently stirs up questions that need to be understood so that effort can be put forth in addressing them. Many family business failures are simply due to thinking things are going to happen naturally, or, worse, ducking the issues that need to be addressed. From my conversations with professionals that engage in helping family businesses, I would estimate that over 75 percent of family businesses that engaged help that is a) qualified, and b) experienced, successfully transitioned from one generation to the next.

## *What if the Time Comes, and the Next Generation Isn't Ready?*

Smart family businesses spend a lot of time and effort to ensure a successful transition to the next generation. Starting early, communicating well, and getting good advice will help with the process. However, what do you do if the age gap between you and next generation is so wide that the next generation is simply not ready to take on the leadership of your company when the time comes? Worse, what if the need to transition hits suddenly due to health or other reasons, and the next generation is just not ready?

Hopefully, you would be around for the transition, and preferably from a porch overlooking a lake, not a hospital bed. But how can a sudden transition best be handled when the next generation may not be ready? Let's look at some strategies.

The main issue here is that there's a gap between when you're willing or able to run the business and when the next generation can pick it up. Two main safety nets that should proactively be put in place for every company, whether a family business or not, are:

**Good middle management**—A strong management team is one of the best strategic planning initiatives any company can undertake. Without strong management, all the power, knowledge and skill rests with the head of the company. Thus, if the head is gone, nothing is left. Case in point: If you're trying to sell your business, the first thing a buyer will look at, after the financials, is the strength of the management. "Having a strong management team in place that is capable of managing the business going forward, without the president, is one of the top factors in increasing the sale price of any company," according to David Boykin, a business sales specialist at Transact Partners International.

Good middle management also provides flexibility in plugging the gap until the next generation is ready. The best alternative is that someone from the company bench could step up and fill the leadership void. However, there are certain characteristics required of such a person – he must have respect for the employees, he must be comfortable that the role is not permanent, and he would be in a role where he would need to actively mentor the next generation. This last part is critical, as the wrong person could do everything to not groom the next generation, or worse, undermine the next generation in an effort to retain the top post.

If it is determined that there isn't a good candidate for the top role, the management team could provide a resource to recruit an interim leader of the company to ensure it continues operating. If the situation requires that the next generation take command, a good management team is valuable in assisting and guiding the new, unseasoned leader.

## Incenting Key Nonfamily Executives

The future success of most family businesses depends, not only on the family successfully leading the company, but also on key, nonfamily executives. As the business grows and multiple generations become engaged, a critical issue to the ongoing success of the business is the ability to attract, retain, and reward key, nonfamily managers to help grow the business long-term.

Here are the key issues:

- Don't want stock to be owned by nonfamily members.

- The compensation program for most family businesses is comprised of salary and an annual bonus with no regard for the long term performance of the business.

- Most family shareholders feel a sense of obligation and desire to share the rewards of the business with key nonfamily executives to the extent they are responsible for its success.

- Some nonfamily managers have prior experience in public companies and would like the opportunity to own stock or receive stock in the business as a form of compensation.

Creating an incentive plan linked to the success of achieving the results of the strategic plan can provide a powerful alignment of interests. Here are some financial incentives:

**Enhanced Deferred Compensation**: Deferred Compensation plans allow select executives to allocate a portion of their regular earnings into the plan to accumulate tax deferred, often in self-directed investment accounts.

**Phantom Stock**: The company establishes a plan setting a cash award event at some fixed point in the future, and makes book-entry awards to the selected executive(s).

**Stock Appreciation Rights**: Unlike phantom stock, whose metric does not necessarily tie to stock price, a stock appreciation right (SAR) by definition is a right granted to an employee to receive a bonus that is tied to appreciation of the company's stock over a set period of time.

**Stock Options**: A Stock Option is a right to purchase the underlying stock at a designated strike price on or before a specified date. The value is tied directly to the value of a share of company stock, but the recipient will have to pay an exercise price in order to unlock the appreciation.

**Restricted Stock**: Restricted stock grants are actual shares of company stock given to executives that are not transferable until certain conditions have been met, such as time in service, or achievement of some predetermined performance goal.

**Performance Unit Plans:** Performance unit plans are similar to phantom stock plans because book-entry awards are made to participating executives upon meeting goals set by the company. These goals are set according to readily measurable executive performance.

**Restricted Section 162 Bonus (Bonus Life):** Bonus life plans differ from the preceding plans in that the asset does not stay with the company. Typically, a bonus is paid to the executive, and the company takes the payroll deduction.

Overall, the keys to successful implementation include:

- Selecting the corporate goals to measure and reward

- Selecting who can participate

- Selecting a plan and measuring its impact

- Communicating the benefits to the participants

A properly executed long term incentive plan will enhance the overall value of any family business and serve as a tool to reward and retain key nonfamily executives throughout their career.

Luther Lockwood, Managing Principal, MBL Advisors, Inc., A McColl Bros Lockwood Company http://www.mbl-advisors.com/

**Board of Advisors** – As I mentioned before, a board of advisors can play a similar role to a strong management team in that they can fill in for an interim period to manage the company. This interim could be until the next generation is ready, or until an outside hire can be brought in. They can also provide direction and advice to the company on the best steps to take considering the situation. They already provide oversight for all activities, so if an internal candidate is chosen as an interim or permanent leader, they can provide guidance and monitor performance. Similar to a good management team, if absolutely necessary for the next generation to step up before they are ready, a good board can go a long way in helping the new leader find his way.

## *Bridge the Gap*

Unfortunately, although you've just read the benefits of building a strong management team and putting together a good board, many family businesses neglect taking these actions. I point this out because if you do find yourself in an emergency transition, there won't be time to slap together a good board or build a strong management team. The alternative is to hire an interim president.

A good interim president can be difficult to find. There are many folks who tout being interim presidents or CEOs, but finding one who can do the work, is available, and fits your budget makes it challenging. Nonetheless, it's the best alternative. A good interim CEO can be invaluable. They typically have seen many industries, have strong experience in all the functions of the business, and can begin adding value from day one. Most importantly, as they are experienced at being a stop gap, they understand, accept and add value to the reason the company has a temporary leader. For example, they often have exceptional mentoring skills. Mike Carlton, an interim CEO for hire who gained his experience through being the CEO of a mid-sized bank for many years, puts it this way: "Effective interim CEOs must be able to quickly assess the performance of a company, understand what the key drivers are and not just work with but develop the potential leaders of the company."

Another viable alternative is to bring in a consultant or a strong general manager. This takes on a little different flavor, as they typically come in and work with the current management as opposed to leading it. For example, I worked with a client that simply had some bad luck at finding an appropriate CEO. As such, we decided to put the search on hold and form a management team that includes the office manager, the two up-and-coming next-generation leaders, and myself. Together, we are the management team that makes decisions and reports to the owners.

## Keep Everyone Informed

Once a course of action has been determined, regardless of the choice, of utmost importance in surviving an emergency transition is communicating to all customers and employees that you are aware of the situation, it is being worked on and operations will continue.

As with all family businesses, however, there are other factors to consider in addition to the business itself: the ownership and the family. For ownership, the best decision is to place majority control with the future leader of the business. Unfortunately, there is not always one clear leader. Nonetheless, it is still a better answer to have one person be the final decision maker, if possible. More companies fail not because they made the wrong decision but because they either didn't make a decision or made it too late. With 50/50 ownership, decision making can be stifled or even shut down. In any case, be sure to have a well thought out and constructed buy-sell agreement in place, so that if either party is unhappy, they can get out.

If you need to be bought out, agreeing upon a practical sales price is complicated. If this is truly an emergency transition, my strong advice is to get some outside counsel to guide the family through this. Otherwise, there may be no more Thanksgiving dinners together if the negotiations go awry.

As for the family element, it's critical to include family members who don't work at the company. When leadership changes hands, control changes. Ownership and money is involved. Thus, all family members will be interested. Establishing open communication from the beginning will help stave off any sense of suspicion that could arise.

Dealing with an early or surprise cessation of leadership in a family business can be a delicate maneuver. If you put too much on the next generation when they're not ready, your business could lose key employees and valued customers - ultimately resulting in the demise of the company. But if you bring in good outside help and heed their advice, your family business could successfully make it through to the other side.

Of course, everyone would prefer to have a clear plan in place to avoid these situations. In the next section, I will guide you through how to plan for succession and manage the transition to the next generation.

# SECTION IV

*Ownership*

# CHAPTER 6

## Choosing and Training a Successor

In July of 2013 the people of England, and reporters around the world, were excitedly awaiting the birth of a rather special baby. On July 22, Prince George of Cambridge was born with a weighty future already on his tiny shoulders. This little prince is in the direct line of succession for the monarchy of Britain, behind his great-grandmother, Queen Elizabeth, his grandfather, Prince Charles, and his father Prince William. Of course, they have to die first.

This method of installing the next ruler of England has worked, for better or worse, for more than 1,600 years. Inheriting the throne through death may be a fine philosophy for royalty of England, Japan, and Monaco. But for a family business, dying at your desk is not considered a good succession strategy. This type of succession typically spells doom for any family business.

Handing the reins over to your son or daughter, and moving into a consulting role while you are still at the top of your game, is a far better plan. Ross Perot, a self-made billionaire may have said it best: "There's no better place to live than in your son's shadow."

### *Where Do I Start?*

Once I presented at a large industry trade show at the Navy Pier in Chicago to a group of family businesses on family dynamics and best business practices. One man in his early sixties had a fairly complex family business situation but had not done any succession planning. After hearing about such a broad range of topics, he seemed a little overwhelmed. Thus his question: "Where do I start and is there a list of questions to ask?"

This is always a concern with the leader of a family business who really has not started the planning process. In my experience, the best place to begin is to simply declare to the family that you are going to begin.

Call a family meeting, close the door, and simply state that the company and the family need to begin thinking and talking about preparing for the future of the business. Yes, you have opened Pandora's Box, but better you than someone else; and much better opened now rather than later.

A critical piece is to include the family. I met a family business leader at a conference a few years ago and he explained to me that he had constructed the ideal succession plan for his family business. When I asked him what the other family members thought of the plan, he told me he had not told them yet. When I suggested he include them in the process, he said there was no need as he had already come up with the perfect plan. (Perfect, except none of the people it affected had any opportunity to discuss the plan or provide input to it!)

I didn't have the opportunity to follow up with him, but I think it is safe to say that he had a rocky road ahead of him.

As for what questions to ask, I had to resort to the classic Harvard Business School answer: It depends.

The concerns facing a large, poorly performing family business with a number of family members not working in the company are not the same as a smaller, high-growth family business with highly skilled family members working in the business. One size does not fit all.

The answer here is to dig a little deeper to understand the real issues, and to gather input from all the key stakeholders. Armed with this information, you can seek out the answers useful for your particular family business situation.

Many family business leaders, especially when they are founders, seem to have a difficult time relinquishing their power. One reason is that they have so much experience running it. They have managed the business successfully for many years and have all the connections with suppliers, the allegiance of key employees, and deep relationships with many customers. After so many years at the helm, they almost intuitively know which button to push and string to pull to move the business forward.

Many times family business leaders simply cannot separate psychologically from the business. While the average tenure of a Fortune 500 CEO is about seven years, the average duration of a family business CEO is much longer--not to mention the many years that CEO has spent in the business prior to leading it, and the countless hours sitting around the family dining table talking about it.

At some point, leaders of family businesses may have lost their own identity separate from the company. The company has become their identity. If they were to step down, who would they be? The thought of leaving could be terrifying.

Jack Welch, the former CEO of GE, may go down as one of the greatest CEOs of all time. However, what secured his legacy was him successfully passing leadership to Jeff Immelt.

The beauty, however, was not in choosing a capable successor, but in grooming him, transitioning him in, and then getting out of the way. Why should the transition in family business be any different?

You have worked hard to build up the business, and it has provided a good living for you, your family, and all your employees. Shouldn't you put forth equal effort to ensure that the business continues to operate effectively after you are gone?

## The FIAT Family Business

As a consultant, I am on the move quite a bit.

As my clients pay my way, I try to travel as affordably as possible. I always fly coach and rent the cheapest class of automobile available. I flew into Philadelphia one time and went over to Alamo (they have electronic kiosks that will get you on your way in about a minute). As I headed over to the economy area, instead of being presented with the typical image-busting selection, I was surprised to find myself standing in front of a little fire engine-red Italian car.

Most people recall FIAT as meaning "Fix It Again Tony" when they left the United States market in 1984. Its true name is Fabbrica Italiana Automobili Torino, and it was founded by Giovanni Agnelli in 1899. Under his guidance the company grew to become the third-largest company in Italy. When his son and heir Eduardo tragically died in a plane accident, the reins moved to Giovanni's grandson, Gianni.

Gianni was known throughout the world as a man's man. He drove fast cars, owned the Italian soccer team Juventus, was considered a playboy, was appointed senator for life, and was named one of the five best dressed men in the history of the world by *Esquire* magazine. Along the way he grew FIAT into one of the largest auto manufacturers in Europe.

With his son Eduardo showing no interest in the family business and ultimately committing suicide, Gianni did not have to search the family bench long to find his nephew Giovanni.

From the beginning, Giovanni showed interest and promise. He was smart and witty, and had a happy-go-lucky attitude. He attended an American high school. His mother was the heir to Piaggio, the manufacturer of all those little Vespa scooters you see in Italy. As part of the grooming process, he was required to spend some time working on the FIAT factory floor under an assumed name. Later he joined Piaggio, where he quickly worked his way up to chairman before returning to FIAT.

However, the characteristic that probably served him best was his humility. When he was in high school at The McCallie School in Chattanooga, Tennessee, one of his best friends did not even know that he was part of the FIAT family for the first year he knew him. I know, because I was that friend.

Gio, as his friends at school called him, was a great soccer player, a top student, fun to be around, and gave off no sense of his wealth or future importance. Around graduation time, I remember asking him what he wanted to do after college, and I vividly recall his saying, "I'd like to go out and make some of my own money before I go to work for my family business."

The highest correlation to a successful succession in a family business is the next generation having spent some time working outside the family business. This helps the heir gain a sense of independence, and to understand his or her place in the world. Gio had already accomplished this at eighteen.

However, Gio did not become the head of FIAT; his cousin John Elkann did. John, the grandson of Gianni, also had an incredible upbringing. He speaks Portuguese, French, Italian and English, has a baccalaureate from France, a master's degree in engineering from Italy, and worked at GE's storied Corporate Audit Program. Today he is the chairman of FIAT, and chairman and CEO of EXOR, an investment company controlled by the Agnelli Family and one of Europe's largest industrial holding investment companies.

Why didn't my friend Gio become the head of FIAT? Tragically, he died of a rare stomach cancer at the age of thirty-three, newly married, with a newborn, and his whole life ahead of him.

Sometime soon you are going to see a cute little Italian car driving around. When you do, take a moment and remember the Agnelli family business and my friend Giovanni.

Then take another moment and ask yourself this question: what are you doing to prepare the future of your family business?

## When to Give It Up

A recent front page article of the *Wall Street Journal* sadly proclaimed the decline in risk-taking among workers and entrepreneurs in the United States: jobs are added more slowly, less money is put into new ventures, fewer businesses are started, and workers are less inclined to change jobs or move for new opportunities.

This avoidance of risk can also be found among family businesses, where there does seem to be a greater reluctance in the next generation to take over the helm of the family business, choosing instead the security of a large corporation.

Family business owners, who dream of one day passing the business on to the next generation, certainly must be asking themselves what can be done to combat this mentality. To do this we first need to better understand what is driving this trend.

In a family business there are multiple pressures on the next generation to take over the business. First is the current owner's desire to see his life's work continue on. Many times when a business is sold it is reconfigured, moved, or simply shut down, all of which are anathemas to the owner. On the other hand, transitioning the business to the next generation can give the owner significant influence to shape the future direction of the company. The message to the next generation that a sale would mean "chopping up the business and only you can save it" can create an uncomfortable position.

The pressure escalates if the family business is a second generation or later business, as there is a desire to continue the family legacy.

And if this is not enough, the next generation has to walk the sometimes thin line of working for the woman or man who also happens to be mother or father.

Finally, the fact of the matter is that sometimes people just do not want the responsibility of running a company. As Tony Raney of

Chapel Hill states in the *Wall Street Journal* article, "I have no desire to show up and be the head of the corporation. I just want to show up and do the job."

Laying the path to a successful family business transition requires a bit of threading the needle. On one hand you don't want to paint an overly rosy picture, as this can create a sense of entitlement, the false perception that running a business is easy, and all you need to do is count the money and show up periodically to check up on things. On the other hand, demonstrating how difficult it is to deal with the business and how much stress it creates will probably not result in your kids lining up to fill out a job application.

Practice and actual experience are some of the most important aspects of bringing the next generation along. Give them summer jobs while they are in high school and college where they can learn the various aspects of the business. Allow them as much responsibility as they would like to have, but don't breach their capacity. As they progress, and when they join the family business full time, find some group initiatives. This will expose them to actually working in a group and seeing group dynamics. This is the first step to developing people and leadership skills. At the same time, give them some individual projects where they are solely responsible for the results. This generates a sense of ownership, and helps them learn to reach out to others for information and help. The bottom line: move them up the ladder as fast as they are willing and able to go, while exposing them to the rung just out of reach.

Finally, be honest. State the opportunity early, but paint it accurately. Yes, it can be stressful, but with better training and preparation than you had, it can be very manageable, and generate a very rewarding life.

## Women in Family Businesses

President Obama proclaimed in a State of the Union address that, "Women make seventy-seven cents for every dollar a man earns." Interestingly, this dynamic may be less prevalent in family-run businesses.

Family businesses come in a variety of different shapes and sizes. But one type of family business that is under-discussed is women-run family businesses. Running businesses has historically been a man's world. But in the 1940s men got shipped off to war and women needed to backfill their traditional work roles here at home. Through this, women came to realize that not only can they add value in the workplace, but they enjoy it, too. Women gained further empowerment in the 1960s through legislation outlawing wage and employment discrimination based on gender. (Not to say that both did not continue in practice.)

Since that time, women have been working hard to break through the glass ceiling. Some progress has been made—women now account for 60 percent of bachelor degree holders in the United States, and run many renowned Fortune 500 companies, such as IBM, Hewlett-Packard, Yahoo, and yes, even General Motors. Unfortunately, women still only make up less than 5 percent of Fortune 500 CEOs. But interestingly, in family businesses they make up over 25 percent.

Women-run family businesses tend to be a business founded by a woman with the husband participating in a support role, alongside a sibling, or by divorced women looking to get back work.

What I have found is that women who run family businesses have an extra burden in that they are still mom at home, and are also mom with their children in the business. To be sure, fathers play a critical role in the life of their children, and love their children just as much as the mother. However, mothers are looked upon as, act as, and dare I say, *are* the primary caregiver and emotional support for their children.

Much of this is environmental and learned, but according to Dr. Louann Brizendine, author of the book *The Female Brain*, brain chemistry and genetic wiring in women actually gear them to be good caregivers and emotional support for children. For example, the larger prefrontal cortex makes women more patient and pacific, larger and more active insulae better equip them to better read nonverbal cues, and their pituitary gland in conjunction with the hypothalamus aids nurturing behavior.

What makes it doubly hard for mothers to run the family business is that their children inherently look upon them as their caregivers and emotional support system. Thus, while mom may be doing a fine job separating business and family, it can be more difficult for the children: they may see their mother running the business, as opposed to their boss. As such, they may not respond well to orders in the workplace from someone who prepared them dinners, bandaged their skinned knees, or tucked them in at night. And the more mom has trouble separating the mother/boss roles, the worse their children's behavior can become.

"It can be more difficult for mothers running a family business, but it doesn't have to be" says Delaine Mead, Owner of the family business Valuebiz. "Most everything women learned about being a good mother at home is directly transferable to the workplace. You have to juggle multiple priorities and treat everyone fairly, but you still need to set boundaries and have consequences for the family or business to function well."

Being a mother is hard. Being a working mom is harder. Being a working mother, leading a company, and managing family at work is incredibly difficult. To make it easier, leave no doubt that you are the boss at work, even if you are mom at home.

## Don't Forget the Mothers and Daughters

The *Los Angeles Times* headline read: "Marines to Make Room for Women on Front Line." Clearly the dial is moving in the quest for equality for women. When it comes to family businesses, women are also viewed as integral to the success of the enterprise, but this has not always been the case. We know that historically, women have not been valued in the workplace. Indeed, at my family's business, Olan Mills, my grandparents had two sons and two daughters. My two uncles joined and eventually ran the business; my mother and aunt were never even considered. We have all heard similar stories.

I had a client in a very male-dominated commodities business. The daughter never considered joining as it was understood that it would not be a good fit. However, she did find herself working in another very similar industry. Having risen to vice president while still in her twenties, with her siblings not stepping up to take over the family business, guess who the obvious successor became?

Much progress has been made for women in business, especially through the 2008 bust in the male-dominated housing industry and the increased demand in the health care industry. In 2010, the overall unemployment rate for women was 8.6 percent, compared with 10.5 percent for men. Indeed, women made up over 58 percent of the workforce in 2010. Similarly, women account for the majority of all workers in the financial services industry, in education, and in health care. And while women do continue to be underpaid, 29 percent of working women in 2009 had more income than their husbands, compared with only 18 percent in 1987. Certainly more needs to be done here.

But women are progressing at light speed in family business leadership as compared to corporate America. According to the American Family Business Survey published by MassMutual, women made up 24 percent of presidents and CEOs in family businesses in 2007, compared with only 5 percent in 1997. But when weighed against the 2.5 percent of women in the top job at a Fortune 500 company in 2007, the difference is stark.

Paige Carter Blair, the vice president of Financial Security Associates, agrees that it can be a tough road. "It was very hard to come into our family business as a young woman, in a male-oriented industry, and for a man, my dad, who is leader in the industry," she said. "However, conquering these obstacles has now made me respected in the business and in the industry as a high performer."

Working for a family business also does have its benefits. Liz Hawley Ennis, who works at her family-owned Eclectic Garden, puts it this way: "Working in a family business with my mother and my sister has been a wonderful experience. Because we all love and trust each other, we know we have each other's back. So we work effectively together. But at the same time, each of us knows that we can take the time outside of work when needed to deal with personal issues. This has been especially helpful raising kids."

Traditionally in the family business the mother has been referred to as the "CEO," meaning the chief emotional officer. Mom has had the role of not working at the company, but acting as the loving mediator between the father and children working together in a family business, trying to facilitate and foster good communication. However, that role has greatly changed so that CEO for women in the family business means chief executive officer.

## *Tips for How to Select the Next Family Business Leader*

So who will lead the family business in the next generation? This is the most vexing question facing any family business owner contemplating the succession task before them.

With the birth rate still around 2.2 children per couple, and cousins and in-laws thrown on top, the typical family business could have multiple family members in the next generation vying for position as the future leader of the business. Moreover, it is highly likely that one or more high-performing employees could be, or want to be, considered to take the helm of the company.

The first default position is to try to not make a decision. There are a variety of ways to do this:

- *Divide the company into parts and let each sibling run that portion.* Unfortunately, it is rare that a company has the size to split up, and even if it does, this would negatively impact efficiencies. More common would be heading up different divisions. However, this still leaves company-wide decisions as shared responsibility.

- *Rotate the leadership role.* Every six or twelve months each sibling takes a turn running the company. This sounds good in theory, but undermines strategy implementation, consistent leadership style, and having one face to the customer.

- *Share the leadership role.* This is really the default situation when no leader is actually chosen. There are many family businesses who manage to run the leadership of the company as a committee. But there are more that fail. The trick is to have a very strong culture of respectful communication, and to truly understand and be OK with the fact that sometimes your idea, despite your passion for it, may need to be given up.

- *Buy another business to allow one of the siblings to run that.* Again, not all family businesses have the wherewithal to run out and purchase another business. A better and more practical derivation of this is to fund the startup of another business. However, this needs to be done in a professional manner with the intention and belief that it can be successful, not to give a child something to keep themselves occupied or keep them out of the business.

- *Bring in or select a nonfamily member to lead the company.* There are two ways this can be done: the right way and the wrong way. The right way is to have a truly qualified professional who is respected in the industry, and by the family members, to lead the company. The wrong way is to put someone in place who is called the leader, but whose job is really to negotiate between the siblings.

But if you truly would like to increase the chances of the family business continuing successfully into the future, a leader should be chosen. As such, the importance of leadership must be discussed and understood. Libraries of books are written on its importance and myriads of historical examples exist to reflect on. And we read every day about the impact CEOs, entrepreneurs, and coaches have on their teams. Equally important, it must be explained that each of the children is loved for who they are, and just because one may be chosen as the leader has no bearing on the parents love for each child. If the company does well, everyone does well.

So how to choose? The best method is to create or obtain a job description for the leader of a company like yours in your industry. While this can be done through interviews, research, and your own experience, bringing in an outside HR professional will create great credibility and impartiality. Once this is established, bringing in outside business professionals to complement the evaluation process can be invaluable. The ideal situation would be to have a board of advisors in place to coordinate this effort.

The final critical element in selecting the next leader to run the family business is to realize that it is not all about who will lead. It is also about ensuring those who are not selected are in support of the decision and can work as a team with the new leader. And remember, maybe the best leader is not one of the family members at all.

## Advice from a Nonfamily CEO

As CEO of a 125 year-old family company I reported to the fourth generation chairman. I was not the first nonfamily member in that position but my few predecessors had grown up with the Chairman. I had been hired from the outside and after a dozen years in preparation I was still to be tested. To succeed I had several essential elements in my favor.

I was an important link between generations. The next generation was in middle management and I could offer the opportunities they needed to achieve their destinies. A prerequisite was running the business well, with particular attention to their growth.

Adding to my good fortune, after his long and highly successful tenure as company head, the Chairman was ready to delegate the business to me and my strong group of senior managers. He was hardly bashful about offering new ideas and certainly critiques, but I was the CEO. How often is the founder and owner of a company capable of giving reign to an appointed head? Note Nike, Starbucks and so many others where intentions to step aside crumble upon the first whiff of not doing it "my way."

Not that I forgot who owned the place. One morning the Chairman appeared in my office to ask a favor. "I know you are against this capital expenditure but I want it and if you will propose it to the board I won't ask you for it again." Made my day but that night I remembered if he wants it again he'll find another to say "Yes."

Underlying it, the Chairman and I shared the core human values that led to our being annually named as one of the 100 Best Companies to work for. The two of us were distant socially and in status, but these shared beliefs created compatibility and credibility.

There were downsides. I had no status in the business world. Successes were family successes. A tough part of my job as a nonfamily CEO in a family company was making organizational choices that had a business purpose but were also timed to the career progression of the next generation. Communications between us were sometimes uncomfortable, but it was important for me to be the positive link between the family and the organization. Later, my successor phoned to say he had no idea how much time I had spent in the Chairman's office.

Several years into retirement I take great satisfaction from my contribution to one of the most successful family enterprises of all time.

Bill George
Former CEO of SC Johnson

## *At the Right Times, Less Leadership Can Be More*

If you are the current generation leading a family business, you might be asking yourself something along the lines of "How do I lead us through this process?" As the leader of the family business, it is your responsibility to chart a course for a successful transition that covers changes in ownership and leadership, addresses estate planning and wealth preservation, and maintains family harmony along the way. While this is sufficiently overwhelming by itself, I'd like to focus on what may be the most difficult part of succession for the current generation.

At first it really didn't compute for me that Jerry Yang, the co-founder of Yahoo, "resigned" from the board of directors of his own company. He was only 43; he had a great company; it's the only thing he knows, and heck—he was the founder! Did he really have that much of a hankering to hit the golf course every day? Of course not--he was fired. Perhaps more delicately worded, he was shown the light.

The number one succession issue facing a family business is the inability of the current leader to make space for the next generation. Part of the problem is that it is so counterintuitive: The way to lead the family business through succession is to *stop leading*. Jeff Krepps, a family systems specialist, describes it this way: "When a child leaves home, parenting must also change. Otherwise the relationship can break down. This dynamic is also present in family business succession, but instead of the parent reacting to the change, they must proactively change their behavior." They need to step back a bit.

Yes, it is incredibly difficult to do. You are the expert at what you do, anticipate issues and opportunities before they exist, and have deep bonds with customers, suppliers and employees through years of battle in the marketplace. But now I ask you, what would happen to your family business if you went on vacation for a month with no phone or email? Or if you got hit by the proverbial truck?

There are some obstacles to "letting go." First, you are so much better at it that the business cannot afford any missteps. But we know that for anyone to learn something, they must do it themselves and make some mistakes. (My wife and I are trying to teach our kids to cook, so we accept that some pans will get ruined.)

The second issue is that they will want to change the business in some way. You are not going to like these ideas because you have either tried them before and don't think they will work, or you lack confidence in the next generation to execute. However, you may want to also consider that you are probably a little more risk averse than you used to be. Family businesses that have grown from one generation to the next didn't achieve this because they sat on the business they were handed. They made some changes. Better the next generation try while you are ready and able to help.

But perhaps the biggest obstacle is that you have become synonymous with the business. People identify you as the company. Thus, relinquishing some control or responsibility of the company begs the question: Who am I if I am not leading this company? This can be a scary thought.

Creating some space for the next generation to step up is not always easy or comfortable. If the company is doing well, why rock the boat? If the company is doing poorly, while you may have a lot to offer, perhaps you are standing in the way of progress.

Maybe this is what someone at Yahoo helped Jerry Yang figure out.

### Show Them You've Got What It Takes to Take Over the Business

Perhaps you are a next generation family member thinking about the future of your family's business. Perhaps you have enjoyed your work in the company so far. You got a bird's eye view into the real operational issues of the business at an early age and privileged access to upper management (a.k.a. mom and dad), and the top management team listens to you. As the next generation working in the business, it would certainly seem that if you stick around, one day this could all be yours. Well, maybe.

As the next generation, it is important to understand that when the current leadership steps down, they're going to want to get some value from the business they've worked so hard to build. There are a variety of options out there: they could sell to a competitor, bring in private equity partners or sell to an internal group of nonfamily managers. For certain companies, setting up an employee stock ownership plan (ESOP) could be another option.

If you are interested in taking over your family company, you need to demonstrate that you are indeed the best alternative. To start, you must have a good sense of who you are and what your values are, and be able to stand behind those values. This means you can remain calm in an environment of disagreement, conflict, rejection and even personal attacks, and think through situations rationally instead of emotionally. You take action and make decisions based on careful thinking and internal beliefs without reacting to pressure from others. You don't succumb to others in seeking approval or force others to your beliefs. What is core here are your independence and the principles you stand behind.

Working in a family business can make it difficult to develop a sense of independence. Since you were born, mom and dad have been telling you how you should live your life, and now that you are an employee, they're telling you how to run the business. Clearly, we all must go through the learning stage, which inherently means you're dependent on the teacher. But at some point, you must assert yourself as capable of operating some or all parts of the business without relying on your parents.

Carry the correct expectations: Don't seek or expect special treatment because you are a family member. Employees outside your family expect you to receive special treatment—prove them wrong. Start at the bottom, and earn your way up. Come in early, stay late, and take on those tasks that need to be done but no one really wants to do. You'll gain more respect and cooperation down the road if everyone knows you've dug the ditches—and will dig the ditch right now if needed.

Competence is twofold: It entails being reliable and dependable, and being able to perform required tasks well. Regardless of the job, you must arrive at work on time, dressed and groomed appropriately. You must be honest and diligent in your work, meet deadlines and show respect and courtesy to employees, customers, and vendors. At the same time, you must perform your job well, and strive to become the best you can be in your role, whether it's in sales, purchasing or customer service.

Seek out feedback from others on how you're doing and advice on how you can improve. Move around to other departments, too, if you can. If you've been in accounting for some time, try moving to marketing. Attend the industry conferences, and lead some of the sessions. Read the industry magazines to take in as much information as you can. Practice continual personal development (CPD).

Become a good communicator. This does not mean talking all the time, but rather establishing an environment where people know they can talk to you about issues, and that you, in turn, keep others informed about your actions and intentions. Others should consider you a good listener. Practice active listening by paraphrasing back to the speaker what they said. Hold or actively participate in meetings, and be inclusive in meetings and conversations.

Once you have established your independence and demonstrated your competence, raise your level of participation in and perspective of the business outside of the functional areas to a more strategic level: Where should we be going with this business? How should we react to competition? How do we prepare to become a better company in the future? Always ask yourself, "What actions can we take to double revenue?"

While each of these areas has an entire college course to support them, these guidelines represent a tried-and-true path to a successful family business succession to the next generation. When the time comes for mom and dad to retire, make it a foregone conclusion that you should be the one to take the company into the future.

## Plan Now for Selling the Family Business Later

Maybe you're an aging business owner with an eye on retirement. Or you're an entrepreneur who has been ready to sell the family business for a while, but you were waiting for signs of an improving economy.

In any case, you are considering selling the family business – perhaps now, perhaps a few years from now. What should you do now to get ready?

You've already accomplished much by thinking along these lines, according to experts. You have been able to overcome the idea of parting from the business. And you are willing to sell to someone outside of the family.

"This might actually be the hardest part of the entire process," says Walter Zweifler, a New York-based financial researcher who has been appraising privately held businesses since 1976 and has consulted many family business owners who have considered selling. "Business owners do not think they will ever die, and have enormous trouble psychologically coming to grips with not owning or running the business."

Now that you've gotten past that part, here are other things you should be thinking about to get ready:

- End the family perks. That means no more sports tickets, toys with motors, or nonworking family members on the payroll.

- Show some profits. Demonstrating strong earnings attracts buyers.

- Get inventory straight, accurate, and current.

- Have an outside party audit your financials so the buyer can trust them.

- Strengthen management. Show that the business can operate without you.

- Get outside help in selling your business. Even lawyers don't represent themselves. If you're a small company, find a business broker through your local chamber of commerce. If you're a larger company, go to a qualified investment banking firm for help finding a certified professional experienced in buying and selling businesses on behalf of people.

Once you have found an interested party, realize buyers and sellers may still have to negotiate to optimize the deal for both sides. For example, perhaps the seller really wants to stay on for the next couple of years, but they found the buyer today. A possible answer to this is that the seller can reduce the price of the company, in exchange for staying on under a three-year salaried contract. That way, the seller is happy, and the buyer doesn't have to pay as much up front.

It is every business owner's dream to see their life's work continue and grow within the family. But maybe, if you are honest with yourself and can overcome the emotional barriers, you will see that the intelligent prep and sale of the business will enable you to leave a financial legacy that will benefit your family for many generations to come.

### *Will Your Successor Be Ready to Lead Well?*

Succession in the family business is undoubtedly the foundational issue of family business dynamics. But when we say succession, do we mean ownership, leadership, estate planning or "What the heck will I do with myself if I am not running this place?"

Once I attended a client's holiday party. It was a nice affair with good employee representation. As is protocol, the owner and founder stood up to thank everyone for their hard work during the year, and then took a moment to recount the sixty-year history of the company. And in closing he made one final announcement: Effective immediately his son would be the president of the company.

What do you think the reaction of the employees was? What do think it would be for most family businesses? Could be good, bad, or ugly. Chances are this declaration would not evoke a unanimously positive response. But in this case there was widespread and sincere applause, cheering, and standing ovations. Why did this passing of the baton happen so smoothly? Because the next generation was ready.

Yes, there are many questions that need to be answered to have a successful family business transition. But lining up the next generation of business leadership is at the core.

There are some key ingredients to developing a successful next generation family business leader.

- *Independence:* Next generation leaders must have confidence in themselves, their thoughts and their beliefs. Much of this can be developed while working in the family business by constructing and leading significant projects. In the case of my client, he began a division, got a loan, hired employees, and increased revenues more than 15 percent. But the shortcut to creating the required mentality is to work somewhere else early on. This is why so many multi-generation family businesses include this requirement in their family business constitution.

- *Competence:* This is more than just being able to do the work. It means developing bottom-up experience. Not just being the accountant, but being able to reconcile the accounts and perform the journal entries. Not just being a sales and marketing manager, but having been on quota and worked the trade shows. IBM, originally a family business, had an unwritten rule that to be a top executive you needed to have spent time working as a sales representative. It also requires that you gain some level of external knowledge and training regarding your function, whether through reading relevant material or attending seminars and workshops.

- *Work with people:* It is not enough to just be smart and confident. You need to be able to work with people. The book "Emotional Intelligence" by Daniel Goleman outlines two studies measuring the success of a batch of high school valedictorians and Harvard graduates. He found that those who possessed the ability to perceive the emotional state of others and react to it in an appropriate manner were much more successful in their careers. The ability to effectively communicate falls into this same category.

- *No special privileges:* Showing up to work on time, staying late, taking on special projects and being measured by the same metrics as everyone else shows that you are part of the team and that you want to be judged on the merits of your work, not your bloodline. This will help the next generation gain the respect of coworkers.

Stepping back, these qualities could simply be labeled leadership. Steve Miller, cofounder of the University of North Carolina Family Enterprise Center, encapsulates it this way: "There are many factors attributable to the success of a family business, but none is more essential than leadership. The difference between those family businesses that succeed and those that flounder or fail can many times be chalked up to the quality of leadership."

In the next chapter, I'll discuss how you can make this transition smooth and be confident that you are leaving your business in good hands.

# CHAPTER 7

# *When Family Isn't the Right Fit for the Future*

The dream of most family business owners is to pass the business on to their children, with the hope that it will continue for many generations to come. My goal is to try to help them achieve that dream, if possible. Unfortunately, some family businesses simply should not go to the next generation. Yes, it can be sad. But trying to force a square peg into a round hole will only create a great deal of damage. Relationships will become frayed, wealth can be negatively impacted, and lives can be wasted.

When the default plan changes, business owners often have much consternation over figuring out a succession plan. However, this does not have to be the case. The fact is that many family businesses are not designed to pass on to the next generation.

If you are running a small retail store and it does well enough to pay for your kids to receive a top-notch education, then most likely your kids will not aspire to come back and run the family business. At the same time, many first generation businesses can be in a field dependent on fast-moving technology or significant creativity. For these businesses, it is difficult to find anyone who can lead the company, making it unlikely the next generation will possess the required rare skills or natural ability. I had a client that fell into this last category.

The founder of the company has an engineering degree from a prestigious university and worked as a senior engineer at Rockwell International for many years. He now runs his own company providing custom engineering solutions. While his children are bright and motivated, none have an engineering background. Given the highly technical and ever-changing nature of the products and services, it is unlikely the next generation will be able to lead the company in the future.

Then there are financial constraints. Consider an owner whose total net worth is almost entirely in the family business. One child is in the business and three are not in the business. Can a parent reasonably leave the entire estate to just one child? Not likely. And if the other siblings do become shared owners, the pressure on the one running the business can be so unbearable that he or she would jump at the chance to sell it.

Another financial scenario is when the number of owners in a multi-generation family business has simply outgrown the ability of the company to provide the jobs or size of dividends desired by the many family owners, forcing the question of selling the business.

However, the most obvious reason many family businesses do not pass from one generation to the next is simply that the next generation has chosen a different career path. If the company is an engineering company and the daughter has her master's degree in psychology, this is probably not a good fit.

All the above "natural events" whittle down the number of family businesses that need to work on figuring out succession. The "unnatural events" are, of course, when your kids are clearly not capable or interested, or are so passionate and skilled they have already taken over and grown the business beyond what you thought possible.

Clear away all of this and you are left with a good chunk of family businesses that truly need to put forth effort figuring out and working through a succession plan. And to this end, it is important for these family business owners to understand the overall objective of succession: Preserve the wealth that has been built up due to the business and retain the harmony among all the family members.

If the wealth of the business erodes, no one will be happy. But if the wealth is retained and family relationships are damaged, that is not success either. Many times we fixate on the wealth aspect, but let us remind ourselves of the importance of upholding family relationships.

## Family Businesses and Families Must Sometimes Part Ways

I am often asked what is more important in a family business: the family or the business?

My first instinct is to explain that this is not really the proper question as it assumes that you can only have success in one area and not both. While sometimes difficult to achieve, you can have family harmony and a successful business.

One place the question often arises is when the family squabbles have become so intense or so intractable that someone declares we should all throw in the towel and sell the business. Sometimes it comes simply because there is no more energy to deal with the issues.

I had a client who would regularly threaten to sell the business when he was not having a good day, people were not responding to his bad ideas, or he was simply not being shown the respect he felt he deserved.

He could not see that he was the problem. The company had grown beyond his capabilities. Because they could not get him to stop meddling and hindering progress, the other family members had decided the answer was to sell the business.

In other instances, the family does not want to discuss or face obvious issues for fear of hurting a family member's feelings. Compensation is out of line, performance or contribution to the company is not what it should be, or someone is really not cut out for the job. Many family businesses choose to overlook these areas of underperformance for the sake of maintaining family harmony.

Certainly, as any parent of young children can tell you, you need to choose your battles. Nothing is ever going to be perfect. But when the performance of the business is taking a dip because a family member is not adding value, should you allow it to continue?

The more common situation is not when the company is in trouble, but when it is simply not reaching its potential. Everyone is getting paid, has plenty of vacation, and the business is making do with 2 percent net profit. Because everyone is "OK," this environment makes it more challenging to instigate the conversation with the family member whose contribution is holding the business hostage.

So answering the question is not as easy as it might seem.

So ask the question another way: What if the business failed and the family succeeded?

If the family business collapsed as a direct result of the involvement, or lack of involvement, of a family member then the only way back to harmony is simple forgiveness. You can't give the business another try; it is gone.

On the other hand, what would happen if the business succeeded and the family failed? Everyone made their money, but no one shares Thanksgiving dinner together. While no one is happy about this, the opportunity still exists every day to make things right.

What we know for a fact is that the most successful businesses are the ones that are run as businesses. However, we also know that those family businesses that have a high degree of trust, and practice open and honest communication, are the highest performing of all businesses. When it comes to family businesses, the whole can be greater than the sum of the parts.

## *Six Signs That It's Time to Sell the Family Business*

Perhaps you have started to suspect you may need to sell your business rather than pass it on. Here are a few indicators that you should consider selling the family business:

1.  **Your children don't want the business.** If you run a small retail shop that put your kids through college, the chances are they have their sights set on bigger goals when they graduate. The harder situation is when the company is big enough to warrant their joining the business, but they just aren't interested. This can be painful when it happens. There is nothing wrong with laying out the facts regarding the opportunity that the family business presents to them. But forcing the company on your children will only result in either resentment or poor performance.

2.  **Your children are not capable.** I have unfortunately had many clients where, despite their hopes and dreams, their child was really not cut out to run the family business. My task was to bring the owner around to that idea. Sometimes there are circumstances where an outside leader can be brought in to run the business. But in that scenario, the question then becomes whether or not the kids can be good owner/managers.

3.  **Ownership has become too diluted.** Unless the company is always growing, it is hard to support a growing number

of owners. This is true whether they work in the business or not, because the company winds up issuing dividends to those not in the business. Also, it could be a struggle to provide sufficient incomes to a large number of active owners. And there's also the increased difficulty in managing the business among multiple owners.

4. **You receive an offer you can't refuse.** This was the situation with Anheuser-Busch, which was purchased by Belgian beverage giant InBev in 2008 for $52 billion. The offer was far beyond the realistic value of the business. And while the old guard tried to rationalize keeping the business, the current generation felt they would be foolish to turn down the offer. Don't try to convince yourself that you are keeping your company for your kids unless they understand the money involved, loudly declare their desire to run the business, and have a credible plan that makes financial sense.

5. **Members of the next generation don't like working together.** Maybe all your kids are capable, but they can't seem to get along with each other. If they are not getting along now, it will only be worse once they are in business together. Rolling the business to them will impact your retirement plans, affect their lives, and possibly destroy any relationship they might have had.

6. **There are major changes in your industry.** Market and technology changes can alter the business landscape such that it requires massive reinvestment to reposition the company. Sometimes it is just not worth that investment.

This is what happened to our family photography business, Olan Mills. People will always want a nice family portrait, but with everyone having a high-resolution camera on their cell phone, the demand virtually collapsed.

You worked hard to build the business up. It would be wonderful if you could successfully pass it on. But sometimes the difficult but smart decision is to sell the family business.

### *Family-Owned Olan Mills Sold After Nearly Eighty Years*

A few years ago, I received an unexpected phone call from my uncle, the chairman of Olan Mills. He was calling to tell me that our family business, Olan Mills, was being sold.

If you are under thirty, you may not have heard of Olan Mills. But if you went to church or school, or had children or were a child in the 1960s, '70s or '80s, there is a very good chance you had your picture taken by an Olan Mills photographer.

My first reaction was sadness. The company has always been at the epicenter of our family and in many ways defined a part of each of us.

But, understanding the photography industry, and knowing that the buyer provided quality photos and valued their employees as Olan Mills does, I am comforted that it was a good sale.

The company was started by my grandfather, Olan Mills, and his wife, Mary. Being the youngest of eleven children on a farm in hard times, he set out to make his own way. Family legend has it that he borrowed a camera from a friend and set up a sign on a street corner offering to take photographs. Five cents down and five cents when you came back for the picture.

A couple came along, plunked down their nickel, and my grandfather took their picture. When they returned the next day, he apologized that the pictures didn't turn out and said he would need to retake them. In reality, since he was broke, there had been no film in the camera - he needed that first five cents to buy the film. I call this American ingenuity.

Realizing he had struck upon something, he began going door to door offering to take pictures. The business grew so fast that he hired as many good sales people as he could find. And at the end of the day, all the sales people would come back to his house for dinner, many staying the night. It was truly a different era.

The true boost came when they began calling people by phone at home. It is a well-hidden fact that Olan Mills virtually invented telemarketing (sorry, everyone). However, it was a different model than what we know today. Olan Mills would use demographic data to know where to set up a studio near a growing residential area, and then hire local employees to work in the studio to phone the lady of the house at appropriate times.

With this model in place, Olan Mills was well positioned to benefit from the baby boom. Studios could not be set up fast enough. The headquarters was set up in Chattanooga, Tennessee, with manufacturing facilities in Springfield, Ohio, and Dallas, Texas.

My grandparents had four children. Their two sons, Olan and CG, joined the company, and their two daughters (one of whom was my mother), did not. Olan Mills II, the oldest child, was in the business the longest. My uncle Olan began running a piece of the company after college. "One of the great aspects of being in a family business is that you have the opportunity to take on big responsibilities early in your career," my uncle reflected.

The company grew to more than 1,000 studios across the country, expanded into the United Kingdom and Canada.

However, in the late 1980s, the company's fortunes began to turn. Telemarketing was getting a black eye because of rampant inappropriate usage, ultimately resulting in the Telephone Consumer Protection Act. This curtailed Olan Mills' ability to directly target new families.

Then digital photography also began making great strides in quality and miniaturization. While an experienced photographer with a high-quality camera can never be replaced by amateur digital photography, millions of cell phone cameras in people's hands will affect demand.

So I am not sad about the sale. Yes, the company where I earned my first paycheck is no more. But it made a good living for my family and thousands of employees, and it provided cherished memories for millions of people for nearly eighty years.

### Blood, Tears, and Whether to Sell

It's rumored that when InBev offered $52 billion to buy the brewer of Budweiser, August Busch IV, the fifth generation Busch to lead the family business, told his father that he really did not want to sell the company, but they would simply be crazy not to accept an offer that high.

I am sure most of us would accept that offer faster than we'd hit the road to the beach if our Friday meetings got canceled. But then most business owners don't have a business worth tens of billions or even tens of millions.

Nonetheless, many business owners suffer through deep consternation when faced with the prospect of selling their business. The simple remembrance of all the blood, sweat, and tears you, your parents and maybe your grandparents spent building this business make it seem like heresy to throw it all away for a wad of cash.

And while some can part with the business and never look back, many others sell their company for a pretty penny only to find that life after business is not what they thought it would be.

While the goal of Family Business USA is to continue the family business to the next generation, some family businesses should not or cannot survive.

When I was in Cape Town, South Africa, a few years ago, I met a gentleman who was running a vineyard on the family farm. While it broke his heart, he knew that there will not be a Sonnenberg in the future running the farm that has been in the family for over 100 years: He and his wife have no kids, and all his relatives have left the country.

At the same time, if your children are happy and successful in careers outside the family business, should you disrupt that? Of course, the harder issue is when your son or daughter would love to have the business, but you know in your heart that they simply don't have what it takes.

There is a unique situation where it is highly advisable to sell the business quickly. This occurs when the owner of the company is the heart, soul, and mind of the business and suddenly dies or becomes severely disabled. In this case, there is typically no one designated or prepared for leadership, and no strong management team.

When the business moves to a wife or child who is not in the business and knows little about it, they are overwhelmed. The longer they wait to sell, the more the business will decline, the lower the value they will receive when they face reality and sell it. Hopefully there was insurance.

At the same time, it would be foolhardy to sell your family business as a knee-jerk reaction to dealing with frustrations such as:

- You are tired of the hassles of the business.

- Your kids are not cooperating with your plan.

- Your sibling sees the business differently.

Yes, these are painful issues, but maybe the business is not the root cause, or perhaps you would be trading one set of problems for another.

Selling a business is not a simple math equation. It is an irreversible life choice.

"The best career, life, and business choices are made when there is harmony and balance between the rational mind and the emotional heart," says Rich Conners, the owner of Primarity Resources. "As such, it is critical to go through a process of capturing, defining, and prioritizing the most critical elements that are of the highest personal value to you and your family, in addition to running the numbers on the value of your business."

Along these same lines, Princeton University recently performed a study which determined that additional income can increase an individual's happiness, up until it reaches $75,000 a year. Then the happiness plateaus. So there is empirical evidence that money does not buy happiness.

So if you are considering selling your business, perform the due diligence on the financial side and get some good advice.

But the advice I would give you now is this: Dedicate the time and energy to understanding and getting comfortable with life after the family business. Selling your family business is a life-changing event. It affects a lot of people, and it is forever.

### The Next Generation Doesn't Want the Business – Now What?

On the other hand, perhaps you are a member of the next generation and are not interested in taking on the company. How should you deal with this? Family business owners can become emotionally attached to their companies. When it comes time for mom and dad to start thinking about getting out, it can be difficult.

For most family business owners, the most desired option is to pass the business on to a family member, especially one who's been working in the business. On a financial note, it is also certainly much easier to handle an estate by passing the business on to the next generation than being forced to sell.

So what does this have to do with breaking the news to your parents that you don't want their business? Everything.

The best way to communicate a difference of desire with someone is to be able to understand their point of view and clearly articulate that to them. Convey to your parents that you've given the matter deep thought, and you're not taking the decision lightly.

You must have good reasons for not wanting to take over the company. But if you've been working in the business for many years, rotated through the departments, been successful and are respected by the employees, you're pulling the rug out from under your parents if you suddenly decide it is not for you.

It's ideal to have open communication from the beginning, letting your parents know along the way that you're unsure about wanting to own the business one day. Tell your parents that you want to work in the business and would like to be paid and promoted according to the contribution you're making to the company, and that you're interested in potentially taking over one day. But tell them you also have an interest in opportunities outside the company. In other words, at this point, you're undecided.

Sit down once a year to revisit the discussion so everyone is on the same page. Be open about your concerns, whatever they may be. Then be prepared: your parents may have arguments refuting your concerns.

The part that will require a steel backbone is to be true to yourself by not letting your parents push you into running the business if you don't want to. It will only result in unhappiness for you—and your parents.

Clearly articulate that you understand the difficult position it puts them in, and you don't want it to be painful and wish it wasn't. Offer to assist with the transition. Ask them to try to understand why you're leaving, and that you're not trying to hurt them. Lastly, give it time. This is an emotional situation—all the logic in the world is not going to placate hurt feelings overnight.

Perhaps your dream job has come along outside the family business. If so, don't leave your parents in a lurch. The right thing to do is ensure you have a good backfill before you depart. Hire someone, train them, and have them stabilized before you leave.

If you've been in the business for a while, understand the business and are well-respected, consider being on the board or establishing one. Plan formal meetings four times a year to debrief the status of the company and provide input. Your parents will appreciate your input and be happy that you're still connected to the business. They may have a small hope that you'll come back (and, who knows, maybe you will).

If you're leaving as your parents are considering retirement, actively assist with alternatives: maybe it's finding a head buyer for the business and leading the deal through to conclusion.

The final factor to discuss are your shares of the business. If you and your siblings outside the business all have the same number of shares, there may not be an issue. But if you have shares that were given in anticipation of your taking over the business, you may need to sell or give shares back to the company. If you want to leave on good terms, arrange for no financial gain on your part and no financial impact to the company.

The best way to say you are leaving: "I am your child, I love you, and I will help you with whatever I can. But this is my life, and I want to pursue my own dreams."

# CHAPTER 8

## Handing Over the Reins

Graduation day, your first real job, your wedding day, the day your first child is born and awards for achievements: These are the milestones of life for many people.

For a family business, the day the leadership passes from one generation to the next is the significant event. There are many ways that leadership can pass from one generation to the next. It can be planned or a surprise; it can be bumpy or smooth. You might envision the handover to the next generation being ushered in with a marching band and a fireworks display. In some cases this is true. But the best way is when you barely notice it at all.

More typical leadership transfer styles are outlined in the book *Family Business Review* (see box below). My favorite example is the Monarch - when the king dies then the next generation can assume control. Usually this is disastrous, with heirs squabbling and the eventual leader trying to adjust to sitting at the desk where the buck stops.

Sometimes an emergency prompts the move. A former client experienced a situation where the current generation had a severe falling out, and the best resolution was to simply move the leadership to the next generation. While it occurred rather promptly, the next generation had been in the process of preparing for the transition.

So it was earlier than planned, but was not a complete shock to the system.

The beautiful successions, however, are surprisingly smooth and as natural as you could imagine. One of my favorites was with a son who had managed each of the departments, and had worked with banks, vendors, and customers. He had taken on significant business issues and opened up an entirely new route to market. He had read the books and attended the conferences.

The idea was certainly out there that at some point a transition would occur. But with his father still at the top of his game, there was no sense of urgency.

It happened during a simple organizational restructuring meeting with the son and the dad. Some employees had left the company, and some people needed to be moved up while others needed to be moved over. In the cascading effect a reorganization can create, the question was raised, "What about Allen?"

Allen is one of those unique employees that you can't live with, but you also cannot live without. He is challenging to manage. "If we move him to the new position, who should he report to?" was the question.

"Well, he and I get along great," the son volunteered. "He could report to me."

That is when I interjected, "Well, then I suppose that would mean we would need to make you president."

There was a long silence before the son said, "Well, I guess so."

To which the dad, after a pregnant pause, responded, "Sounds good to me."

And it was done. The leadership had just changed hands.

People often ask me how you know when the best time is to change the leadership. The answer is simple: when everyone is ready. We'll discuss how to set yourself up for this change in leadership, with tips for making sure it is done right.

## Five Ways to Approach Your Exit

As I've written before, much of the focus on family business transition is on whether the next generation can and will step up to the challenge. To be sure this is important; if you are stepping out of the business and there is no one assuming the leadership role of the company, everything you've built may go to dust. Let's assume that the next generation is motivated and qualified to take over the business. In this case, the only thing standing in the way is *you*, the current business owner. The standard retort I hear from the current generation is, "Yes, I want to take some more time off, but I still want and need to be involved in the business. I don't want to just be cast out." It is important to understand that in many cases the immediate departure of the current leadership would be quite detrimental to the future success of the business.

There is a quite simple but effective strategy of transitioning out of the business: start taking every Friday off. It gives you a three-day weekend and allows the next generation a little space to find their leadership footing. After some time of doing that, start taking Thursdays off also. Keep heading in this direction until you only come into the office late every Monday morning to have a cup of coffee.

However, also consider the following five approaches to exit strategies, from Jeffrey Sonnenfeld and P.L. Spence in the *Family Business Review*, as you think about your exit plan.

1. **The Monarch.** How does the king transition power to the next generation? He dies. This certainly is the most risky method of family business transition. Certainly, this is not a method that is thoughtfully and proactively selected as a business leadership transference strategy. Rather, it stems from the current leader's unwillingness to relinquish control, even though there will be negative consequences for such action. If the next generation is not capable of assuming leadership, elevate someone internally who is, bring someone in from the outside, or sell.

2. **The General.** At a predesignated date not of their choosing, generals are asked to retire. However, they may not be personally ready, or still believe that they have value to add—or, worse, believe that no one can do it but them. This is common in family businesses. Mom or dad will go travel, play some golf, and either grow bored or elicit responses from their old guard that the next generation is not cutting it, thus setting the stage for them to come back to the rescue. And then they go away and come back, and go away and come back again, thus scuttling the opportunity for the next generation to get leadership footing.

3. **The Ambassador.** This exit style is commonly associated with highly functioning family businesses. Say dad was progressively taking a day off a week until he was only coming by on Mondays

for coffee. What would also happen is that when there were big contracts out for bid, a major issue at work or simply opportunities or issues that were based on past relationships, dad would arrive in a suit and tie ready to lend credibility and grease the path if necessary.

4. **The Governor.** This style is effective in larger organizations. It also works when the current generation truly does want to get out of the business and move on, or to break company homeostasis, forcing the next generation to step up. Set a firm departure date in the future, then begin working toward making everything happen by that date. While GE is not a family business, this was the famous exit strategy used by Jack Welch.

5. **The Inventor.** This style is where the leader gives up lead of the business but still contributes in the particular area he can offer expertise.

Dirty little secret: More than 65 percent of family businesses fail to make it to the next generation. This leads us to believe that the fault and blame for the failure is completely on the next generation. *It's not!* The current generation has at least 50 percent responsibility as they either hang on so long the next generation never gets quality time in the driver's seat or so long that they start making bad decisions that damage the company.

### *Now Is the Time to Plan Your Exit Strategy*

Say there are two brothers and the wife of one of the brothers running the family business together, and all are ready to get out. The next generation is coming along, so once they get there, how will the three members of the current generation know when and how to leave the business?

Clearly, the first hurdle is financial. Does the business generate enough profit or have enough assets so that it can fund retirement? This depends on how much wealth you think you need for the rest of your life. If the business is generating no profit, has no assets that can be sold or downsized and you're taking $60,000 in salary, you will be hard pressed to sell the business to anyone at a price you can retire on.

Once you've passed that hurdle, ask yourself and the other owners, "Do we want to see the business continue into the next generation?" This is different than, "Am I OK with the next generation owning the business?" There needs to be a true desire on behalf of the current generation to see the business passed to the next generation. We are assuming, of course, that the next generation is ready, willing and able to take over the business. The time this question needs to be asked is when there is a financial need to extract some value out of the company in order to fund retirement.

Now, let's say my personal financial dreams are quite different from my spouse's or brother's. What to do? This is where good communication and a good financial planner are essential. With a husband and wife team, it's vital to go together to a fee-only certified financial planner. These are professionals who have experience doing the math on your current personal wealth, business assets, income and spending wants and needs through life so you can be confident that you will have enough money after you exit the business. Going together is important so that you work from the same set of information to discuss what type of retirement you desire.

The fly in the ointment can be the third partner. His financial objectives can be different from yours. This is where negotiation, compromise, and respectful communication are essential.

There are nonfinancial objectives as well. The biggest one is how you will be affected by no longer being the person in charge of the company. There is an enormous amount of self-esteem and activity that comes with running a company—even more so when it's a company you've built. Many business owners sell, only to find that financial independence doesn't really satisfy the psychological need to be a part of something. Rich Connors, Founder of Primary Resources, is an expert in helping business owners work through selling their business. According to Connors, "There are four aspects that must be considered when considering selling your business: your life goals, your future living, the company legacy and exit readiness."

Along these same lines, you want to be sure that all the stakeholders in the business are pleased with the transition or sale. How will the transition of the business affect your employees, especially the long-term ones? How will it impact the community? How will it impact your broader family?

When there is more than one owner, exiting can be tricky. If both want to leave, who should leave first? Usually, this is solved by circumstances: one of the owners wants or needs to leave now, and can. From a desired sequence perspective, all but the true leader should exit first. This allows the rest of the organization to stabilize before the exit of the leader.

Another tricky aspect of transition, often encountered in family businesses, is when there are two or more siblings in the business, and the leader is simply ready to get out. In this situation, it's common for one of the other siblings to take a shot at running the company. But this typically doesn't work out well, so is not a rational decision when the wealth and livelihoods of many people are at stake.

A better method is to allow the next generation, if they are ready, to assume control while the other siblings continue on. This minimizes the number of transitions and the disruption each causes and gives great support to the next generation leadership, enabling long-term success. (With this said, there have been many family businesses where the siblings or spouses are both at such a high skill and leadership level that one could leave and the other could easily take over.)

One factor that sometimes comes into play is when there are multiple siblings, each with multiple kids. This is when family businesses get tripped up. Each parent is going to want his child to do well and succeed. And any parent would assist his child in finding a job by referring him or her to a friend or acquaintance who is hiring. When it's your business and you're doing the hiring, recuse yourself from the process. However, this isn't practical day in and day out. This is why older and larger family businesses need to become professionalized. While a "family bonus" at the end of the year may have been acceptable in the past, if all the siblings are trying to give their kids the plum assignments, increase their pay, pushing for their promotion and going light on their performance reviews, a train wreck is waiting to happen when it comes time to figure out which current generation members can leave the company.

## *Passing the Company On to the Next Generation*

The first question to ask yourself: Am I selling or giving my business to the next generation? More likely than not, you are selling, but at a favorable discount. There are two types of valuations you can have performed on your business: one to pass it on to the next generation (lower), and another to a strategic buyer (higher).

What if I am passing it on to more than one heir? This can also be awkward, and family businesses unintentionally set up the next generation to fail. It is a best practice to have the leader of the family business with a majority ownership over the others; however, this would depend on the heir being different enough to allow this. Many parents are unwilling to structure the ownership this way because they are uncomfortable explaining this to the potential minority shareholders. However, if you don't give slightly greater control to the clear leader(s), you could stifle the business and create frustration among the owners.

Dirty little secret: When working through succession, and even when simply operating a family business, many family businesses get tripped up by neglecting or not paying full attention to family members who are not in the family business. When thinking of succession, when thinking of estate planning, you must fully consider the ramifications on those family members who are not in the business. The baseline is that if the business were sold, and there was only cash in the bank, the estate would be divided equally among your heirs. It does not necessarily have to be exactly this way when there is a big asset like a business, but failure to fully address the financial and psychological needs of those who do not work in the business can set up the family business to hit a brick wall down the road.

There are instances where the heirs are sufficiently cooperative, in addition to being willing and able, so you can give them equal ownership, or where all of the wealth is wrapped up in the business and this is the only way to provide equal wealth. In any case, it is imperative that a good buy-sell agreement is established.

A good buy-sell agreement will enable a dissatisfied business partner to get out of the company and receive a fair price for his shares. It will also ensure that ownership is not sold out on the open market, and it protects the other owners from potentially being in business with another owner's wife or heirs if one were to die. In the case of a death, life insurance can provide a good liquidity cushion.

The greatest benefit a buy-sell agreement provides is the peace of mind that if things were to go awry, you could safely get out of the business. Interestingly, having this knowledge keeps many sibling partners working together successfully over the long term.

## Buy-Sell Agreements Can Help Family Businesses Survive

Operating a business with your brothers, sisters, and/or cousins is one of the most complex arrangements. Indeed, sibling or cousin family businesses can inherently last a long time. As such, just as good fences make good neighbors, good buy-sell agreements make good sibling/cousin family businesses. Think of it as a pre-nuptial agreement before getting into business together.

The purpose of the buy-sell agreement is to document the details of what will occur if one of the parties dies, becomes disabled, wants to get out of the business or is forced out of the business. The most common concern is the death of a partner.

If a partner dies, then without a buy-sell in place, the ownership would pass over to either the partner's spouse or heirs. If you think your brother's wife and kids are wonderful people, but you don't want to be business partners with them, make sure the ownership passes back to the corporation or to the remaining owners.

But because that ownership may have substantial value, the spouse or heirs should receive their due. The best way to handle this is to have life insurance policies on each member of the buy-sell such that liquidity can be available for the heirs.

At the same time, if the partner's contribution was equal to his share ownership, then the company will be affected by having lost a key employee, which means he will be difficult to replace. Having some additional liquidity to buffer this would also be advisable.

Another key scenario is when one or more partners is a minority shareholder because those shares are subject to a minority discount upon sale. Thus, it is very important to establish a valuation method for a buy-sell. James Duggan, an attorney who specializes in buy-sell agreements, said there are really five ways to do this:

- Agree to a value, but adjust annually

- Agree to a formula to determine value

- Use a certified appraiser, or multiple and take an average

- Value equals insurance proceeds

- A combination of all of the above

However, from anyone's perspective, it is critical to talk through all the ramifications of ending a business relationship before putting a buy-sell into place, especially when there is more than one partner involved. With only two children per generation, there could be at least four members of the family business in the third generation. While there are templates available and standard scenarios exist, each business and business relationship can be different. Be sure you all sit down and have a constructive family business meeting. What you want to avoid most of all is having to execute a buy-sell and find out that it does not accurately convey what your original intentions were when it was put into place.

The next consideration: Who am I passing the business on to, and who am I not passing it on to? The best answer here is always to try to pass it on to those who work in the business. In order to foster greater success to the next generation of leadership, it is best to ensure they have control over the business.

One of my clients had a general manager who held only a minority of the shares, and none of the other family shareholders worked in the business. Under these circumstances, if the company wasn't performing to the level desired by the outside shareholders, they might start sticking their noses in the business in an effort to improve it, knowing nothing about it. And if you are a C corporation, it can be more awkward, as dividends would be the only way to pay the other shareholders. Thus, the owners would also be forced to take dividends, when dividends are double taxed and the owner's salary may be more than sufficient.

If you have sufficient other wealth, it's best to simply equalize gifts of stock to those working in the business with cash or other assets to those who are not working in the business. If you don't have the wealth, then a good life insurance policy can create enough liquidity at your death to enable those in the business to inherit it and those who are not to receive the cash. Without some liquidity, the financial pressure on those in the business may be so severe, they are forced into a panic sale.

If you are selling the company to those working in the business, you don't have to completely equalize with their other siblings, unless you're selling the company at a lower value than if you were to sell it on the open market. What is critically important is to ensure all family members are aware of what's going on so no one is surprised later on. Having a good family meeting can alleviate all of this.

## *Finding the Funding*

So now you are lined up to move forward. Where is the money going to come from? There are a variety of options.

1. **Leveraged recapitalization:** The company can take debt from a lender, using company assets as collateral, and buy out a portion of the shares of the owner. With a private equity firm, their interest will be in building up the value to have it resold. However, the next generation heirs can also buy them out.

2. **Joint venture:** Bring in an operating partner. If they bring the skills, vision and money, this can be a good option.

3. **Noncontrol investment:** Sell a minority ownership stake in the company. If your business has a good track record of making a lot of cash, there are investors out there for whom this would be a good investment. But they will want a tight contract, and so should you.

4. **Sale over time:** Having the next generation buy out over time is probably the most common option. This, of course, necessitates that they continue to run the company well so there is cash available to buy out the owner. Many times, the next generation can be forced to take out a loan to make this happen.

With any financial option, it is critical to clean up the books as much as possible. Have a strong financial person, have the books audited and get all nonworking children off the payroll.

> ## Estate Planning Is Essential
>
> According to Stephen Rhudy, an estate planning specialist at Walker, Lambe, Rhudy, Costly & Gill, the absolute most important part of estate planning is to actually do some estate planning. "Procrastination is the deadly sin of estate planning, as we know that over 70 percent of people who die do not have even a will in place." Many family businesses can also benefit from the implementation of a revocable trust.

### *Show Them You Can Lead*

As part of the transition, the current generation must allow the next generation to establish themselves within the business while they are still involved. Are you looking to take over a family business soon?

One of the crucial elements to your success as the next generation managing the business is your ability to win over all constituencies: customers, suppliers, employees and partners. You know the product and services. You've mastered the core functions. You've successfully and independently led significant projects and initiatives to completion. You've spent time being mentored by someone further down the road. You've had some advanced training and education in the industry. And, optimally, you've spent time working outside the family business. However, none of this actually connects you to the groups of people with whom you must have strong relationships in order to be successful.

A client of mine, a second-generation family business in construction, had developed a reputation for being the best. The two children in the business had the skills, knowledge and motivation to be leaders in the company. But the real success of the business, the "secret sauce," if you will, was the strong relationships the current and previous generation leaders had developed with their partners and suppliers. In many ways, the success of the business depended on these relationships, the business network. In order for the next generation to be successful, they needed to begin gaining the network's trust to garner the benefits of good relationships.

The best approach to developing any relationship is to feel each other out. Carve out a bite-sized portion of responsibility for a project or a less critical function, and have mom or dad inform the customer or supplier that you will be handling this area. This enables the customer or supplier to feel out your performance quality without assuming all the risk. It's important to avoid communicating this change in the relationship yourself–it would convey the customer's or supplier's relationship with the current ownership is not important enough to warrant a formal handoff. As the next generation, you would also run the risk of appearing arrogant and overconfident by announcing your own takeover.

The customer or supplier doesn't care how much you know until they know how much you care. You may be good at what you do, but the road is littered with people who were good yet couldn't connect with people. Being good at what you do is not enough to develop a strong relationship with customers and suppliers. It's more important to prove, establish and develop a reputation for how you work—that you're reliable, trustworthy, dependable, communicative and caring. The critical thing to remember is that you only get one chance at a first impression. If you can win over your customers and suppliers by over delivering on small projects, they will be comfortable when you move to bigger responsibilities, and will cut you slack if something happens to go wrong because you've already built some trust.

While there needs to be a transition period where your parents can introduce you as taking over some responsibilities, you certainly don't want to seem like dad's sidekick. Prove that you have the capacity to stand on your own two feet and think for yourself. Set up one-on-one meetings with customers and suppliers to discuss topics relevant to them. The seriousness of the work is not as important as demonstrating that you're not just an extension of your parents and operate well independently.

Along similar lines, plan on attending some industry conferences solo. Look for opportunities to write published articles on industry topics, and speak to or teach groups. Just getting involved in industry-related initiatives demonstrates you're not a one-trick pony. It also gains you exposure.

Perhaps the most important aspect of helping your customers and suppliers see you as the future leader is to reach out to them directly. For a supplier, it can be as simple as taking the initiative to call and invite him to lunch or coffee to discuss ways to work more closely. For customers, staff the front door and greet them as they walk in. Introduce yourself and ask if you can help. It's a tried-and-true method of establishing a reputation as someone who cares. You could ask customers how you can be a better provider for them. Sure, there are a myriad of projects to be worked on, personnel issues to address and crises to avert, but carving out a few days to meet customers will be worth the results. You can't meet and help everyone, but it has a meaningful impact on those you touch, and they'll spread the word.

Finally, as you set out to make your own mark as the future leader of the company, remember one thing: While your parents may have a particular style that endeared them to their customers and suppliers, no one expects or wants you to be their clone. Yes, everyone wants reliability and quality products and service, but they also want trust and sincerity. Be yourself, have your own style and double-down on your own strengths. This is the best way to advertise to your customers and suppliers that there's a new leader on the way.

## *When the Baton Is Passed, Are You Ready To Run?*

As the up-and-coming next generation leader of the family business, there are many things that need to be done in order to smoothly transition the business. Some are not so obvious.

First, let's discuss what we mean by "transfer." From a business perspective, we tend to keep our eyes on the business and who currently owns it. This makes a lot of sense as, prior to the handoff, the business is and has been in fine, capable hands. So let's take a quick look at the receiver, or the next generation owner.

Just like in a relay race, the one with the baton does not want to let go until she is sure the receiver has a good grip on it. This is exactly how the current generation feels, too. However, the handoff, in this sense, occurs over years. You need to prove that you are capable of running the business before the owner lets go.

There are a few questions that need to be answered to determine if you are ready:

- Do you have a sense of independence? There is a saying that it is lonely at the top. Well, it is. There is no one to talk to about decisions you make. Certainly, there is plenty of input, but ultimately you must make the final decision. Can you say no in the face of strong opposition? Do you know what your values are? Have you said no to your father, mother or whomever is running the business? All of this is required to be a leader.

- Are you fairly good at what you do? If you are in a financial business and are not good with numbers, maybe the family business is not for you. But if there are aspects that appeal to you and others you are weak in, spend time working to understand those aspects.

- Are you a good communicator? Can you speak and write fairly clearly? Are you confident when communicating in person? Can you tell people things they really don't want to hear? At the same time, do you understand the importance of communication, and can you ensure that it happens on a regular basis?

- Are you thinking ahead? Where should the business be three, five or ten years from now? How should we get there? What needs to change? In business, the ground underneath your feet is always changing. Can you keep up and even get ahead?

- Are you evolving? Are you constantly seeking out ways to improve yourself and be a better manager and leader? Are you a good listener? Do you seek out advice? Have you initiated a major project and seen it all the way through to completion, rising above setbacks?

The list can go on, but the point here is that the current generation is always evaluating you and will be looking at these types of characteristics and actions to get a feeling for how prepared you are to take over leadership.

The next area involves lining up other external parties. Do your siblings and other key employees support the transition of the business over to you? You need to find out where they stand and what concerns they may have. In any business, there will be some highly qualified managers who have a good relationship with the current leader. You may have siblings who either work at the business or receive income from the business. They will want to know their situation will be OK if you move into the leadership role. If they need to be moved out in order for the next generation to be successful, you will need to work all of that out.

The biggest issue to air out is what to do about mom or dad. From your perspective, it may seem as simple as, "Let me have your office." However, you need to truly appreciate the difficulty of stepping down. As such, it is important to define, over time, what your parents will be doing with themselves once they are not fully engaged in the company. This brings up the following three questions: What role do they have in the business? What leadership roles will they have in the company after the "baton" is passed? What do they plan to do outside of work?

While these questions can seem easy, they are not. Remember the issues we discussed with the various CEO exit styles.

The final steps in the transition revolve around retirement planning and ownership transfer. Needless to say, it's important that your parents have sufficient means to care for themselves. This can be handled through keeping dad on to pull down a salary or buying him out. In the case of many family businesses where real estate is involved, rent can be paid for the facilities.

However, the most important aspect of transference is to get the topic on the table as soon as it makes sense. Many family business owners struggle to leave the business because they are so emotionally wrapped up in it, they have trouble seeing their children try to run the business, and they have trouble letting go enough to allow the next generation to make the changes to the business.

It's difficult for many family business founders and owners to relinquish their spots at the top of the mountain. Much of how people are remembered is by what they did at work. It becomes who we are. Letting go of this is tough. I had a client for whom we were simply trying to do some smart estate planning by moving over some assets to the kids. Even though he would lose no control and it would have zero financial impact, he still felt like he was "getting kicked to the curb."

As for ownership transfer, the question is: Is there sufficient wealth or life insurance that would allow those who work in the business to inherit the business, while the other siblings receive cash? If not, then you need to plan for your inactive siblings having some ownership in the business. The best way to prepare for this is to have a meeting with your siblings, without your parents, to discuss everyone's perspective. Try to come to a unified agreement on how you would manage the relationship in the future, and present it to your parents.

The greater sense you can convey to your parents that everything is handled on a personal, emotional, business and family level, the easier the transition will be for everyone involved.

### Ownership Transfer: Financial Considerations

When the time comes to transfer ownership, the standard method is simply to value the business and have the next generation buy the company, but this is easier said than done. Many times, the value of the business is beyond what the next generation can afford to pay, even over an extended period of time. A good question to ask is, "How much money do I actually need from the sale of the company?" There is a spectrum of answers, from, "I need all the money. This is how I'm funding my retirement, and if the next generation doesn't get funding, then we need to talk about selling," to, "I don't need the money, and

I'm going to give away as much as I can without incurring a hefty tax burden." Most companies fall somewhere in between.

We had a client where the current generation bought the business from the founding generation for less than what the business was worth. The founder wanted to see the business get to the next generation, and while he needed some retirement money from the business, he didn't need all of it. Ultimately, the number was a valuation that was as low as possible without alerting the IRS that there was a gift that would require tax.

It is important to understand the difference between capital gains taxes and income taxes. As the capital gains tax rate is much lower than the income tax rate, if you were planning on sticking around the company and continuing to pull in an income after the sale, don't. You and the business would be better off bumping up the price of the stock and lowering the amount of income you'd receive in the future—the best answer would, of course, be none.

In certain industries, there is the added issue of the land the business sits on. Many times, the land is worth more than the business itself, or, at least, is quite valuable. However, depending on the type of business, moving locations can be damaging to the company. This is a common issue in many family businesses· having a valuable asset that, if sold, could fund a nice retirement, but will rip the heart out of the business. A possibility here is to simply buy the business and land over time.

It is important to consider what you're leaving to your children who are not in the business. If the next generation is buying the business and all the assets at a true market value, then there is nothing to discuss. But, to the degree that you manipulate the value down or gift part of it, you need to consider how you will balance this with your other children. This is when a good life insurance policy can be the answer, creating liquidity for other family members.

In many family businesses, the next generation consists of more than just one child. How will you handle two children of equal skill levels and contribution to the business? Certainly, one answer is 50/50. However, sometimes this can sub-optimize the operations of the business if two people have to agree on every strategic decision. Another alternative is to give a slight majority to one, but then put a good buy-sell in place to ensure the minority can get out at a fair price if desired. You can even make a cash gift to the one who receives the minority to compensate.

The point here is not that you love one child more than another, but that the business will operate better with a final decision maker, making everyone better off.

There is a family business I know of where the founders gave 100 percent ownership to one son, even though two other sons were working in the business. The business is doing great, and the three brothers all get along wonderfully. Clearly, the owner son is such a high performer that his two brothers realize that if they line up behind him, they will also do well—and they have.

So where does the money come from to buy the business? Typically there is a buyout over time, with perhaps a chunk up front. Sometimes the business has to shrink a bit in order to fund the buyout. However, there are other options: the bank or private equity. If your company has had little debt and consistent income over the years, and can demonstrate that the next generation has already been running the business, a bank may lend the money to be paid back over time. Another option: If there is an interesting growth plan, you may try securing private equity. This type of arrangement will certainly have a higher payback threshold, but if the growth prospects are good, financially it can work out. There are private equity firms out there who specialize in lending to family businesses with the end goal of getting the business back into the hands of the family.

Another option is an employee share ownership plan (ESOP). Essentially this is a qualified retirement plan through which employees receive shares of the corporation's stock. The benefit of an ESOP is that it allows the shareholder to sell shares to the ESOP entity and avoid taxes, and the company can borrow money through the ESOP and then repay the loan through fully tax-deductible contributions. These tax savings can be significant. However, ESOPs are expensive to set up, so the value of the company has to be large enough to make it worthwhile. At the same time, the company needs to be profitable in order to gain from the tax savings. Finally, the seller's time horizon has to be long enough to benefit.

### Financial Considerations for the Next Generation Owner

For the next generation owners, there are also financial considerations. What steps do you need to take to assure the transition of the business from the first generation to your ownership is as smooth as possible? There are a number of important things to consider.

First, you should get a professional valuation from a certified expert to help you understand how much the business is worth. This doesn't necessarily mean it is the price you'll pay for the company, but it does provide an external and impartial value of the business. And this isn't the only reason a professional valuation is important.

The IRS will want its piece. Let's say the business is worth $10 million, but mom and dad only charge you $7 million. The IRS views the $3 million difference as a gift with possible taxes due. Then, let's say your parents have died, and the IRS does a review and discovers the discrepancy. Guess who pays the taxes? You. Guess who won't have the liquidity at the moment? You. Guess who is forced into a fire sale of the business? You guessed it: you!

The good news is, there is a recognized range of valuations. For example, the value of a business to a strategic buyer would bring the highest value. A strategic buyer is a business that needs another business to complete its portfolio, enter a new market or block a competitor from getting into the market. Think of Microsoft buying Skype for $8.5 billion, even though Skype lost $7 million the previous year and had about the same amount in debt. Microsoft didn't want Google or Facebook to get their hands on Skype.

Through a more simplified financial analysis, without strategic buyers waiting in the wings, how much is the business worth? Get a valuation from a certified professional, and inform them that you need the valuation for the purpose of transferring the business to the next generation, you. That way, if the IRS has a question, the onus is on the valuation professional to justify the price.

As I mentioned before, if the plan is to be co-owners with your siblings or anyone else, it is wise to establish a buy-sell agreement with a valuation process defined. This way, if it turns out that someone wants to leave the company, the separation process will already be understood.

If your parents are financially secure, it's in their best interest to get the purchase price as low as legally possible. Then, they can gift you up to the maximum tax-free amount, and pay gift tax after that level.

Another critical step in understanding the financial ramifications of buying the company from the first generation is developing solid financial skills yourself, as the new next generation owner. The best way to gain these skills is by spending a stint as the chief accountant, with the responsibility of generating the monthly financial statements. If this isn't possible, sit down once a month to review financial statements in detail with your CFO, and attend some financial statement analysis courses. You should also get advice from qualified financial professionals, but considering the importance of the topic, having your own understanding is critical.

As a part of this process, you will need to reconcile how all the siblings will be treated. For example, if they are in the business, how should ownership be divided? Remember, equal is not always better. Also be sure there is a good buy-sell agreement defining the terms under which any owner can sell shares of the company. It can save your business and your relationships. If they are not in the business, then ownership usually should be avoided if there is sufficient liquidity to balance out any gifts. One way to assist with this is for the current generation to have adequate life insurance.

The next step in preparing to take over the business is to be involved in the estate planning of your parents. In many regards, this is the last step in the development process. There are two critical elements for this to go smoothly: having the relationship, trust and healthy communication to be involved and having the knowledge to assist. When it comes to the relationship, it is vital to understand that you may not see eye to eye with your parents on their needs and desires after they retire or when they die. It can be a delicate situation.

Assuming you have the relationship to be involved in the estate planning process, get yourself up to speed with the various aspects of estate planning, including insurance, investing, tax ramifications, and legalities.

There may be other family members involved in this process as well, including siblings in and outside the business. The estate plan will need to treat each sibling in a fair and equitable manner. Business ownership is a key area to consider. If a family member is not working in the business, it doesn't mean he should get shares of the business because he is family. This is only considered, usually, if there is no other liquidity available, or the liquidity available is too important for the growth of the business.

Now, after all this, you'll likely still need to buy the business from your parents. If they are financially secure, it's in their best interest to get the purchase price as low as legally possible. Then, they can gift you up to the maximum tax-free amount, and pay gift tax after that level. However, if your parents aren't financially independent, you'll need to purchase some or all of the business.

I mentioned some funding possibilities earlier, but another exotic funding mechanism is a "captive," which involves setting up your own insurance company to fund the insurance needs of your company. You can own or partially own the insurance company. Over a period of time, the insurance company can shut down, leaving the owners with the proceeds with extraordinary tax savings. Again, this is highly sophisticated and shouldn't be entered into lightly.

Finally, if you don't have a board of advisors, put one in place. Get three to five people who are fully independent of the company and its stakeholders but have knowledge that can be helpful to the business. At least one member with strong financial experience would be wise. This will provide you with a good sounding board as you go through the transition process, from a business, family and financial perspective.

# SECTION V

*Generation Next*

# CHAPTER 9

## Setting Up New Owners for Success

The day has come when it is time to change seats. Perhaps the transfer of ownership is a smooth transition, in which your mom and dad take on different roles and step away from the day-to-day. Or maybe it happened suddenly, even under sad or unfortunate circumstances. Whether the move happened gradually or suddenly, there are steps that need to be taken right now in order for your company to move forward and prosper. In this chapter we'll look at strategies for a next generation owner to successfully take on the family business.

### Get In the Know

Get good financial information and understand it. You are in business to make a dollar, and the measuring stick to determine profitability is your financial statement. If you do not have a good accountant and good accounting practices, fix it now. Building a business on bad financials is like building a house on sand: It doesn't matter how good the house is. It will always have problems. At the same time, make sure you can read the financials well enough to make informed decisions. They are the control panel of your company. If you don't understand them, take a managerial accounting course.

In terms of on-the-job training, the first step is to do a good rotation through the company departments. Instead of just flipping through, read a good portion of each chapter. This will give you the opportunity to see how the business works as a system.

But it's not just about the business process; it's also about the people: the colleagues you work with, the vendors who supply you with the products you sell and, most importantly, the customers who buy the products you sell. Get to know and understand each of these groups, finding out what's important to them.

The next step is to get deeply into the industry. From a learning perspective, it is critical to attend trade shows and conferences. There are three major learning opportunities at industry events. First, meeting with vendors can help you understand all the products and services available, and compare the options. Next, keynote talks and seminars are designed to train and educate you about the various facets of business. Finally, other company operators are on hand to answer questions or discuss any challenges you may have in your business.

Work on your continual development. You must continually educate yourself. It's easy, after many years of being in the business, to think you've seen it all and know everything. But ongoing education is essential.

Reading is one simple step you can take. Magazines are good because they give you quick information. Read industry-specific titles, as well as general business magazines like *Bloomberg BusinessWeek*. In addition, pick up business books about business strategy, marketing, other industries, or other related topics. They could spur broader and more strategic thought on actions that should be taken at your company.

Course work is another avenue you could use to build your knowledge. If you want to be successful running a company these days, it is best to have some business education. If you have an undergraduate degree in business, that should suffice, but if you don't, consider an MBA program. If this isn't possible, take these five courses: accounting, finance, operations management, marketing, and economics. Don't neglect small courses on topics where you lack confidence or those of special interest to your business.

Networking groups are also helpful resources that can produce valuable information from your peers. If you are under the age of forty-five, seek out the YPO (Young Presidents' Organization) group in your area. Otherwise, think about joining a Vistage executive coaching group. Both cost money, but they enable you to share your leadership challenges with other leaders. Then there are standard networking groups like Rotary and Chamber of Commerce. Toastmasters is also an excellent resource to improve speaking skills.

Seek outside advice. Networking groups will take you a long way, but they can only go so deep into your particular situation. Many business leaders, especially newer ones, find benefits in enlisting the help of business coaches, consultants, and mentors. Jack Welch, the revered former leader of General Electric Company had a personal business coach so that someone sharp, who didn't work for him, would talk to him straight.

### Own Your New Role

*Realize you are the leader now.* This means a few things. Congratulations are in order for you, but now is not the time to rest on your laurels. On the contrary, this is the hard part. Up to this point, you were simply a passenger in the car—now your hands are on the wheel. You are in charge, and the buck stops with you. Remember, it is lonely at the top. Smart and experienced people will give you advice, but ultimately it is up to you to decide.

*Accept that mistakes are OK.* Many leaders get hung up trying to either be perfect or appear perfect. This can create an environment where others feel that they, too, must be perfect, and they could take steps to cover up their mistakes. The goal of a business is to make money, and the business landscape is always changing. You need to always be improving, which requires some mistakes.

*Establish your own contacts and relationships.* To get your company to where it is now, your parents or the former owners had a network of folks they would rely on: CPAs, lawyers and insurance brokers, as well as others in the industry and some outside the industry. You don't have to jettison these relationships. In fact, you should keep them all, but you need to determine for yourself who you are going to rely on for information and advice.

*Hire the best.* One of the best famous pieces of business advice is to hire people smarter than yourself. Similar to being willing to make a mistake, this requires putting your ego to the side.

*Plan your time wisely.* Remember, your time is valuable, so manage it effectively. Take the time to train people so that you can delegate. Try to structure your day so you can focus on certain activities in an allotted time frame: e-mail for an hour, return phones calls for an hour, etc. Multitasking allows you to touch many things shallowly. Focus enables depth, which yields higher quality work and is ultimately more efficient.

*Make your company about the people.* Remember that business is about people. Create a sense of team. Motivate and encourage people, and allow them a chance to voice and deploy their ideas. The more people feel a sense of ownership, the more they will go the extra mile. Remember your emotional intelligence—gauge the feelings of others, be aware of your own, and be sure to listen.

## *Leadership Is Key*

But let me shift gears. My intention is not to teach you how to run a business, but how to become a good owner. The difference is the owner is singularly responsible for the company and everything about it.

There are a myriad of theories, books and courses on leadership development, but I'm going to condense it down to nine important elements.

1. **Communicate.** Listen first, understand, then ensure the right frequency and depth of communication with everyone you depend on and who depends on you. Consider Toastmasters International, a nonprofit organization designed to assist in developing public speaking and leadership skills. I also recommend you read *Emotional Intelligence: Why It Can Matter More Than IQ* by Daniel Goleman. The author delineates five crucial skills of emotional intelligence, and shows how they determine our success in relationships, work, and even our physical well-being.

2. **Admit mistakes, and accept criticism.** It is imperative that people are willing to tell you what you don't want to hear, and that you listen to them. Arrogance does nothing for you or your business.

3. **Plan ahead, prioritize and focus on the important, not the urgent.** I recommend you read *The 7 Habits of Highly Effective People* by Stephen Covey. The author presents a holistic, integrated, principle-centered approach for solving personal and professional problems.

4. **Develop people skills.** Business is people, and you need to be able to motivate them to help you.

5. **Work on 360-degree continual growth: mind, body, spirit, and business.** You should always be reading a nonfiction book. Also, make it a point to read a general interest magazine (like *Time*) and a business magazine (like *BusinessWeek* or *The Wall Street Journal*) regularly.

6. **Cast a broad net, and seek leadership opportunities.** Always network, and not just in your industry. Try your local chamber of commerce, church, Lions Clubs, Rotary, and other nonprofit organizations.

7. **Carve out a piece of the business and manage the entire entity from a profit and loss (P&L) responsibility.** It doesn't matter as much where the responsibility is as having the responsibility.

8. **Be proactive, but patient.** There's a difference between taking action and being overly pushy or demanding. In the same breath, there's a difference between not paying attention and waiting for something to develop. It's a delicate balance.

9. **Have an open and ongoing dialogue with the current (or past) owners.** They are in a different stage of life and have different priorities than you. As such, it is important to have honest communication about their goals and your goals, and how each of you see a transition evolving.

Becoming a successful owner is a process that never ends. By learning through the right training, education and experience, you will get there.

## *Keeping Sibling Relationships Positive and Productive*

Perhaps you were not the only sibling to be given ownership of the company. I have a client with three second-generation family members in the business: one is the president and the others are vice presidents. How do they manage to get along, cooperate, and ensure the business is functioning at peak performance? It's tricky. Here are some strategies to keep your sibling relationships strong and your business moving forward.

1. *Put the past behind you.* Unfortunately, some adult siblings harbor resentment for events that happened while they were children growing up, and they carry this baggage with them when dealing with their siblings. They pull these past incidents out as weapons whenever discussions get heated. It's similar to unhealthy marriages, where one partner pulls out the other's past misdeeds and wields them as weapons during an argument. These past misdeeds need to be addressed, forgiven, and put in the past for good. If you want to get along better with your brothers and sisters, you must do what is necessary to get past your childhood differences.

2. *Open communication is the key.* The next area of potential conflict comes when there is confusion over responsibilities. When siblings are acting like owners, they can tend to jump in where needed. However, if everyone is

jumping into today's problem, nothing else will get done. At the same time, if two people are separately working the same issue, there is redundancy of effort, wasted time and ultimately frustration as only one solution to the problem can be used and the other loses out.

I believe the number one factor in developing a good healthy sibling relationship in the workplace is communication. Organize regular meetings, and allow siblings to put whatever they want on the agenda, including personal issues. Always leave time for discussion at the end for anyone to raise issues. Be sure to take turns leading the meetings. When conflict arises, practice active listening: let the other person speak, then tell him or her what you believe was communicated, and ask if you understand correctly. It's important to understand that people cannot move on to the next logical point in a discussion if they're not convinced the other person has perfectly understood the previous point they were trying to make. And remember, understanding someone does not mean you agree, just that you understand.

3. *Assure fair compensation.* Another area that causes rifts in family businesses is—you guessed it—money. How much is everyone getting paid? This is an issue particularly when it comes to siblings who are running the company, as there is no arbiter. Individual self-esteem and psychological makeup of the siblings is greatly affected by the unquestionable love and support received from their parents. Even though they may be completely different people, they're equal in the eyes of their mother and

father. But in the workplace, things don't work this way. The successful performance of the company is most important, and to a great extent, that performance comes from the people working there. The employees with better results will shoulder more responsibility, and should have the appropriate title and compensation to go along with it.

The benefits, however, should be the same, including for those that are not necessarily in the company. Think of a family's second home, for example. Dennis Jaffe, one of the great family business authors, believes the vacation home is a good indicator of family health. Who gets how many weeks, is someone using it more than another, does one want to sell, does another always leave it a mess without fixing anything? It's easy to see how conflict could result, so it's important that the rules are the same for everyone. When it comes to the business, the big issue is vacation days.

4. *Recognize long-term goals.* As a final coping tip for working with your siblings, it is critical to have an understanding of each one's life goals and ambitions. Where do you want to be in five, ten and fifteen years? Life changes a lot as you go through it. People get married and have kids, kids grow up, hobbies and passions come along, and good and bad life-altering events occur along the way.

As we go through life, our perspectives on what we want and need changes. Check in with your siblings to see where they are on their path. Share your hopes and dreams for life with them. In doing so, you'll ensure you are all working together in a way that will allow each of you to get what you want and need out of the business and the family.

## Four Must Reads for Next Generation Leaders

Hey second-generation leaders, you're about to get an educational crash course for success. This turbo boost requires you to read four books that will prepare you to be successful as a family business leader and in life. This is your homework assignment: Go buy and read each of these books:

1. *Emotional Intelligence* - This first must read covers the importance of emotional intelligence, a concept first coined by Daniel Goleman, who has since gone on to be declared a top 10 influential business thinker by *The Wall Street Journal*. In his book, Goleman describes how those who are most successful in business and life have a high degree of emotional intelligence - namely, self-awareness, emotional control, empathy, and the ability to influence others. Our societal structures dictate that, to be successful, we must make good grades in high school to get into a good college in order to get a good job. While this is still true, we have come to realize it's simply not enough - we must demonstrate emotional intelligence as well.

2. *The 7 Habits of Highly Effective People* - This highly acclaimed title from Stephen Covey covers the more

traditional and fundamental skills and know-how required in business. You must read the book to really learn all seven, but the overall concept is to structure your behavior so that you will be successful. Habit No. 1 makes the most impact, I believe - be proactive. Think about this. Most of us in the workplace are passive. We can do it tomorrow or simply react when a problem or opportunity arises. Along the same lines as being proactive is to "do it now." If you have decided a course of action, ask yourself, "Why can't I implement this decision right now, today, this very moment?" Many times, you will find there is no reason why you can't start today. No, it won't be perfect, but speed conquers perfection. Don't confuse being proactive with being busy. This is a major mental fallacy - just being busy or doing physically taxing work is not being proactive.

Habit No. 5 is first understand, and then be understood. Convince the speaker you understand, and then speak. Family businesses are breeding grounds for conflict. Manage it with effective communication. Habit No. 7 is sharpen the saw - never stop learning, growing and accepting change.

3. *Kids, Wealth, and Consequences* - Family businesses are businesses that your family actually owns. Thus, mom and dad set the direction and direct employees on their course of action. They are in control, and have the power to hire and fire people. The livelihood

of the employees is in their control. Moreover, as owners, mom and dad reap the benefits of the profits. This environment can have a psychological effect on the next generation in that they may come to believe they're superior to those around them due to the family's power and wealth. Or they may think simply that they're the children of the one in charge. In actual fact, the parents' position of power has come about through extremely long, hard and smart work. This book guides you, as the next generation, through financial, intellectual and spiritual/emotional choices to assist your development into a well-balanced adult.

How many family businesses get into trouble because someone in the family thought they deserved what they hadn't earned? There is a family business where a father passed on his business to his two sons, naming one president. Unfortunately, the president was driving the business into the ground while ignoring the input from his father and brother. When this son decided to default on a company buyout payment, the dad had no choice but to seize the company back.

4.  *Steve Jobs* - Rounding out this portfolio of must reads for second-generation business leaders is the new biography about Steve Jobs, the late cofounder of Apple. This book is a massive case study of the

earlier three books, and far beyond them. Let me be clear here - it is not a book on how it's done, but rather it shows the good and the bad. The author says Jobs told him to write whatever he wanted, and he would put no constraints on it. This is probably the first time Jobs ever did that, and you can immediately see that it's true. Jobs' behavior through much of his life, as chronicled in the book, was nothing less than abhorrent - not to deny that he is a creative genius who brought the world many wonderful things.

It is a full exposé on leadership styles, interaction and effectiveness. It is unparalleled on motivation, innovation and creativity. It covers multiple aspects found in the books *Emotional Intelligence* and *The 7 Habits of Highly Effective People*. I would contend that the Jobs biography will soon become required reading at some of the top business schools around the world.

You'll notice these reading suggestions aren't hard core family business books. One deals with family and wealth, but the others have no direct family content. That's because the major elements of success for you, as the next generation family business leader, are more fundamental - have feelings, be structured, earn your way and have passion, even if you have to break the rules sometimes. hh814dd.

## *Don't Ignore the Need for Self Improvement in a Family Business*

The dynamics of family businesses are complex and have broad reverberations. If you have managed to work your way through this minefield and have succeeded in passing the torch on to the next generation, you can consider yourself a gold medal winner in the family business competition.

However, the race does not end there.

When I worked for IBM there was an understanding that all employees should make a concerted effort to improve themselves. There were courses available inside and outside the company, an extensive library, and compensation to purchase business books. Self-improvement was so expected that "personal development" was part of everyone's annual performance review.

Yes, I understand that a multibillion dollar company can afford to allocate such resources to employee improvement. But this is missing the point: personal development is important. And for the family businesses it is easily forgotten, ignored, or put aside.

Family businesses tend to be insular. Most are privately held and thus are not held to the same reporting standards as a publicly traded company. More relevant is that most of the critical data and information is reserved for the inner circle of the owners, founders, and/or family. This attitude of not letting information out of the inner circle creates a similar myopia about letting outside information in. Indeed, this insularity, particularly if the company has been successful in the past, can create a belief and mindset that the business philosophy of the inner circle is superior to anything else out there, and external information and counsel are shunned.

Some of this is justifiable, if you truly are the market leader. However, there is a difference between ignoring outside education, advice, and information, and bringing it in, evaluating it, and determining which parts may be useful and which are not.

We met with a family business a few years back to discuss how we might provide help. After a couple of hours it became clear that both the family and the business were highly functioning and succession was proceeding very smoothly with everyone on board. We determined that they really did not need any help, and applauded them for having a discipline to always be on the lookout for ways to improve.

Look at Jack Welch, ex-CEO of GE and considered one of the great leaders of a great business. Nevertheless, while at the helm at GE he retained a personal business consultant just to keep him on his toes. If one of the greatest leaders of an iconic company needs help, don't you?

So you are the new leader of the family business, but the transition has occurred rather early. As such, there may be some experiences and perspectives you need to gain in order to fully equip yourself to be a successful leader in the future. For example, here are some questions to ask:

- Are you truly willing to accept constructive criticism? Are you willing to admit when you are wrong or have made a mistake? Have you dealt with conflict?

- Have you been in a situation requiring perseverance? Are you a good listener?

- These are experiences and attitudes common to good business leadership. If you are already at this point and consider yourself a fairly well-seasoned leader, do you take seriously the concept of continual personal development?

Do you read self-help business and industry books? Take course work specific to your industry? Belong to leadership groups like Vistage or YPO?

- Do you spend some time with a business coach? Have a network of mentors? Attend Toastmasters to improve your public speaking? Participate in business groups like the Chamber or Rotary?

If you are a new family business leader, you may believe that you have sufficient experience and education, and the success of the business proves it. Or you may think that you are too small, too busy, or don't have the resources to spend time improving yourself. You would be wrong on both counts.

## Conclusion

There can be no greater joy than successfully owning and running a business where you get to work with the people you love the most. At the same time it can be very lucrative and provide a fulfilling life. Unfortunately there are a myriad of obstacles that impede so many family businesses from achieving this point.

Most of all, it is the inherent blending of business with family. Business is a bottom-line, profit driven, no holds barred competition to perform and evolve better than your competitors in providing products and services to the marketplace at a value point that customers are willing to pay for and generate sufficient profit at the end of the day. Families are the exact opposite—they are a broader extension of who we are as individuals. It is our clan, it is our core group, it is where we always belong, it is our refuge, and it is our home. And it cannot be changed.

Dirty little secret: This is where family businesses go awry. They are unsuccessful in maintaining adequate balance between the demands of the business and the needs of the family. It is like a bicycle, if one wheel is not operating fully, then the entire enterprise does not properly function. We must pay sufficient homage to both sides of the equation, each of which has polar opposite requirements. Moreover, while there is certainly an art to being successful in business, dealing with relationships is a fuzzier and more amorphous issue to tackle. This is probably why so many family businesses are now reaching out for help.

The purpose of this book has been to enable those family members connected to a family business to get a deeper look at the underlying mechanics of what makes a family business work and not work that are not typically discussed at cocktail parties. As mentioned at the beginning of the book, every family is different, and thus the answers to successfully moving forward, while there are certainly some best practices, are unique to each family. The cookie cutter approach is wholly ineffective. I am hopeful that some information contained within the book resonated with you and your family business.

Finally, let me conclude with two final parting "dirty little secrets" of dealing with family business issues. Many times we either know that something is just not right, but we can't figure out what, or we are faced with such a complex family business issue that we go crazy trying to figure out the right path forward.

Next to final dirty little secret: Your employees -- especially ones that have been around for a while, the senior ones, and the really good ones -- they know what many of the issues are. However, they are not going to tell you. They know that speaking the truth could put their job in jeopardy, now or somewhere down the road. At the same time, family members -- especially long-time owners -- are mostly unable to hear it from an employee. It is an "emperor has no clothes" situation.

Final dirty little secret: When you find yourself wound up in knots trying to figure out how to solve a complex and seemingly intractable family business situation, try to step back and, for a moment, imagine that none of these people are related to each other. Now how would you solve the problem? This perspective can provide enormous clarity. This is *not* to say this is the answer, but it can assist greatly in constructing a solution that ultimately works for you, the business, and the family.

# ABOUT THE AUTHOR

Henry Hutcheson is the founder and president of Family Business USA, and specializes in helping family businesses and privately held businesses improve business operations, prepare for transition, secure wealth, and strengthen family relationships.

With twenty-five years of business management and family business consulting experience, Henry has successfully helped families across the US and internationally, and in a broad range of industries. While his focus is on succession, his work entails managing conflict and enhancing communication, planning and preparing the family and business for a smooth transition to the next generation, grooming the next generation as high-performance leaders, and working with the exiting generation to define their role going forward.

Henry grew up working for his family's business, Olan Mills Portrait Studios, had an international management career with IBM, UPS and Sumitomo Electric, and now works with family businesses across the globe.

Henry studied Psychology in Switzerland, has a BA from the University of Texas at Austin, and earned an MBA from Columbia

Business School. He is a Certified Family Business Advisor (CFBA), a Certified Management Consultant (CMC), serves on the board of the Carolinas chapter of the Institute of Management Consultants and is a past regional board member of the Society of Financial Services Professionals. He is also a member of the Family Firm Institute.

Henry is a frequent speaker at professional, university, and corporate-sponsored events, was a family business columnist for the *News & Observer* and the *Charlotte Observer* newspapers, is the current family business columnist for the national magazine *Nursery Retailer*, and the Columbia newspaper *The State*. He has written for *Family Business Magazine* and has been quoted in the *Wall Street Journal* and *Crain's*, as well as in various business and trade magazines across the country. He has also been quoted in two family business related books: *Kids, Wealth, and Consequences* and *Sink or Swim: How Lessons from the Titanic Can Save Your Family Business.*

\*\*\*

Made in the USA
Charleston, SC
22 October 2014